27 CHAIRS

DATE DUE			
FEB 25.1998			
GAYLORD			PRINTED IN U.S.A.

Best Furniture Projects
from the British magazine *Woodworker*

27 CHAIRS

Edited by Victor J. Taylor

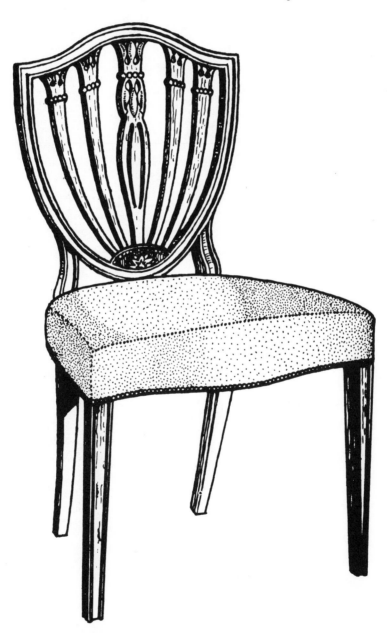

An International Craft Classic

The Taunton Press

©1989 Argus Books

First printing: January 1990

First published in Great Britain by
Argus Books
Argus House
Boundary Way
Hemel Hempstead
Hertfordshire HP2 7ST

International Standard Book Number: 0-85242-987-8
Library of Congress Catalog Card Number: 89-51320
Printed in Great Britain.

...by fellow enthusiasts

The Taunton Press, Inc.
63 South Main Street
Box 355
Newtown, Connecticut 06470

Phototypesetting by Photoprint, Torquay, Devon
Printed and bound in England by Richard Clay Ltd, Bungay, Suffolk

Contents

1 Captain's Chair 1
2 Child's High Chair 5
3 Child's Rocking Chair 8
4 Windsor-Style Child's High Chair 11
5 Nesting Chairs for the Nursery 15
6 Modular Stacking Chair Units 18
7 Swivel Chair 21
8 Mini Folding Chair 26
9 Hepplewhite-Style Chair 30
10 Gimson-Style Ladderback Chair 35
11 Chippendale Library Chair 38
12 Peg-Legs and Sgabelle 43
13 Country-Style Hepplewhite Chair 48
14 Ladderback Chair 53
15 Writing Chair 55
16 Windsor Stick-Back Chair 58
17 Farmhouse Kitchen Chair 62
18 Dining Chair with Drop-in Seat 66
19 Contemporary-Style Dining Chair 69
20 Dining Chair with Laminated Bends 73
21 Dining Chairs with Upholstered Backs 76
22 Carver Dining Chair 79
23 Contemporary-Style Carver Chair 83
24 Turned Oak Dining Chair 86
25 Dining Chair 90
26 Chair with Hide Seat and Back 93
27 Two Modern-Style Dining Chairs 98

27 CHAIRS

Introduction

"Chair-making is a branch generally confined to itself, as those who professedly work at it, seldom engage to make cabinet furniture . . . The two branches seem evidently to require different talents in workmen, in order to become proficient. In the chair branch it requires a particular turn in the handling of shapes, to make them agreeable and easy . . ." So wrote Thomas Sheraton, the world-famous designer in 1803, and his words are still true today.

Changing from making cabinet furniture to making chairs means adopting different techniques, but they are not so different that any capable woodworker cannot soon learn them. You will find all the various skills fully described in this book, together with details of how to upholster chairs, how to steam-bend timber, and other helpful processes.

Over the 80-plus years of its existence, the *Woodworker* magazine has published a vast array of chair designs, and we have carefully selected from back numbers as wide a range as possible – from period styles to those in the most modern idiom, and from children's chairs to special stack-away and folding types. The ever popular and ageless Windsor style is particularly well represented by such examples as a child's high chair, a traditional farmhouse kitchen design, and several others; you'll find it difficult not to start making one straightaway!

Each design is fully illustrated with working diagrams and has a cutting list to make things easier. Whether you're a home woodworker or a professional, you'll find the book a constant source of inspiration and information . . . HAPPY CHAIR MAKING!

—Victor J. Taylor

CAPTAIN'S CHAIR

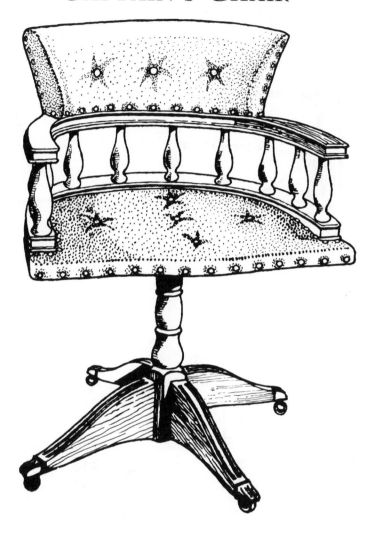

A Captain's chair is a lovely-looking piece of furniture. It can really brighten up a dull room and, besides its aesthetic value, it is also very, very comfortable.

The name derives from the fact that similar chairs were used by the captains of the Mississippi steam boats in the 1870s, and my design is a free interpretation of the original style. The chair is not difficult to make but it does involve some intricate procedures, the most time-consuming pieces being the two U-shaped arms, which are laminated.

ARMS

In order to make these, you must first of all construct a former. A series of blocks measuring 7⅞in by 2¾in by 1⅜in are screwed on to a piece of blockboard, and the inside curve of the arm section is marked on them. The blocks are then removed, cut to shape, and screwed back on as shown in Fig. 2.1.

The next step is to cut the timber for the arms. Sapele mahogany was used for this chair, but any good quality hardwood would do. Eighteen pieces, each measuring 52¾in by 1³⁄₁₆in by ³⁄₁₆in are needed – nine for each arm. Each set must be heated before bending; ideally, they should be put in a shallow tank

of boiling water. You can make up a home-made bending apparatus as shown in Fig. 16.2, Design No 16 but, if this is impossible, a bath tub with three inches of very hot water will suffice. After steeping in the water for about five minutes, all nine pieces are removed quickly (wear gloves for this – they will be hot!) and cramped to the former using blocks of wood and G-cramps.

After two days the cramps can be removed; the pieces should now be, and should remain, basically U-shaped. Apply PVA adhesive to them all once they have thoroughly dried out and cramp them to the former; care must be taken at this stage to ensure there are no gaps. Once the adhesive has set, the arms may be taken out of the cramps, their ends trimmed square, and their surfaces planed flat.

The edges are then decorated by cutting grooves along the sides and ends and you can use a spindle moulder, a router mounted in a routing table, or a scratch stock for this operation; see Fig. 1.3.

SEAT

This is made from three pieces, each measuring 22⁷⁄₁₆in by 8¹⁄₁₆in by ¾in. They are dowelled together before being sawn to shape.

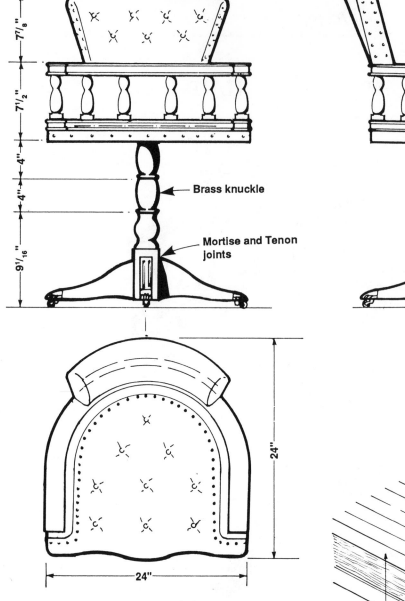

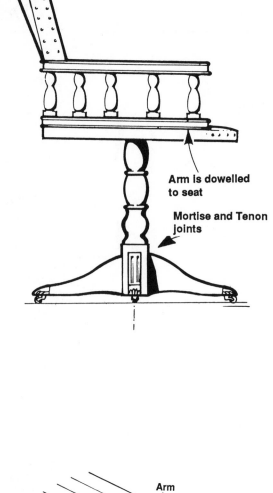

Brass knuckle

Mortise and Tenon joints

Arm is dowelled to seat

Mortise and Tenon joints

24"

24"

Fig. 1.1. Front and side elevations, and plan.

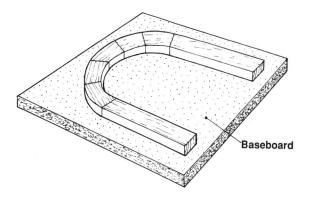

Baseboard

Fig. 1.2. Former for arm laminations.

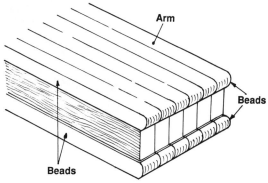

Arm

Beads

Beads

Fig. 1.3. Detail of beads worked on arms.

SPINDLES

These are turned between centres from 6¹¹⁄₁₆in by 1⁹⁄₁₆in square pieces to the shape shown in Fig. 1.1; you can, of course, alter the shape if you wish.

LEGS

Made from four pieces, each 12¼in by 4¾in by 1³⁄₁₆in. The joints are cut first and then a template is used to draw the shape; see Fig. 1.4. A small amount

of wood is left at the tip of each leg to allow for the fitting of the brass claw castors. The two decorative grooves can be made in the same way as on the arms.

CENTRE POST

My pattern consists of three sections – two wood and one brass – as shown in Figs. 1.5 and 1.6 but there are, of course, alternative methods. Making the post requires using a universal chuck and a 20mm sawtooth cutter.

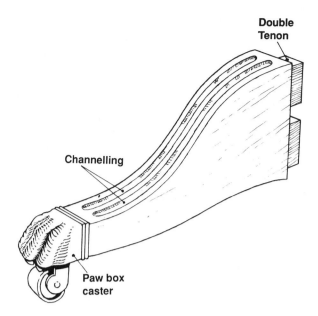

Fig. 1.4. Detail of leg.

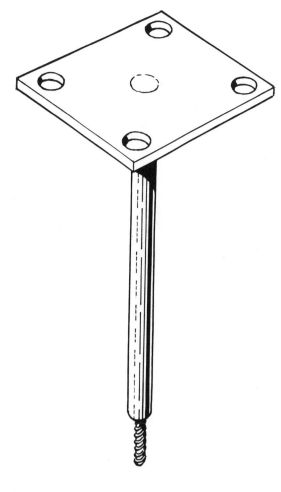

Fig. 1.6. Steel post.

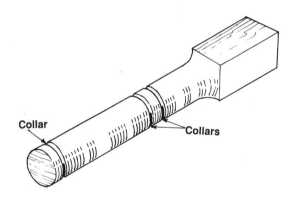

Fig. 1.5. Centre post.

The first step is to take a piece of mahogany, 14⅝in by 1⁹⁄₁₆in square, and mount it between centres on the lathe. The first 5⅛in is left square while the remainder is turned until it is just cylindrical. Four tapered grooves are then cut in the positions shown in Fig. 1.5 to accept the collars of the universal chuck, and you must be sure here to get a tight fit.

The post can be shaped as shown in Fig. 1.1, then taken off the lathe and cut in half. Each half is next re-mounted in the lathe using the universal chuck and drilled from either end with the sawtooth cutter. The base of the square section should also be countersunk to make room for the washer and nut of the steel pipe. Finally, the two wooden sections can be pushed on to the steel pipe and mounted between centres for truing up and glasspapering.

BRASS KNUCKLE
This is surprisingly easy to make. It is first mounted in the chuck and drilled out to 20mm, then mounted on the steel pipe and turned between centres. A normal scraper will turn the brass down to a suitable shape quite easily.

BACK SUPPORT
The upholstered back support can be made from any suitable pieces of wood (not necessarily the same as the remainder of the chair) since it will eventually be covered completely. Fig. 1.7 shows its construction.

ASSEMBLY AND FINISHING
The seat is attached to the post by a brass plate which is silver-soldered to the steel pipe as shown in Fig. 1.6. If you find it difficult to get a brass plate, then a steel one welded to the pipe will do just as well.

It is far easier to finish each piece individually before assembling them with a PVA adhesive. I used polyurethane varnish and obtained an excellent finish by rubbing down with wet-or-dry paper between coats, finishing off with steel wool and wax to tone down the gloss to a satin finish.

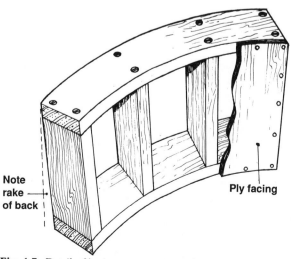

Fig. 1.7. Detail of back support – note 'rake'.

UPHOLSTERY

This is not difficult and no-one should lack the courage to attempt it. Start by cutting holes for the buttons in the plywood facing on the back, and through the seat. The buttons should be the ready-covered bifurcated type, which have two 'legs' (these were called 'snapes' in the old days) – the legs are pushed through the holes and bent back on themselves to hold the button in place.

Then cut out a piece of 2in thick plastic foam to shape, bevelling its upper edges, and stick it to the seat with a fabric adhesive. Next, cut a piece of leather to shape, allowing an extra ¾in or so all round so that the edge can be doubled back on itself. Tack through this double thickness on to the front edge of the seat and around the back curve, and finish off by tapping in dome-headed nails to cover the tack heads. Finally, cover the underside of the seat with a fabric such as black canvas.

Provided you take time and care, you'll be delighted with this robust, goodlooking, and comfortable chair.

CUTTING LIST

	INCHES			MM		
	L	W	T	L	W	T
2 arms	54¼	5⅜	1³⁄₁₆	1353	137	30
3 seat pieces	23	8⅜	¾	584	213	19
10 spindles, each	7⅛	1⅞	1⅝	182	48	42
4 legs	12¾	5	1³⁄₁₆	324	127	30
1 centre post	14¾	3⅜	3⅛	375	86	80
2 back rest rails (ply) from	24⅛	12⅛	½	613	308	12
4 supports, each	8⅜	1½	1³⁄₁₆	213	38	30
1 wrap-round (ply)	28⅛	8⅛	⅛	714	207	3

Working allowances have been made to lengths and widths; thicknesses are net.

CHILD'S HIGH CHAIR

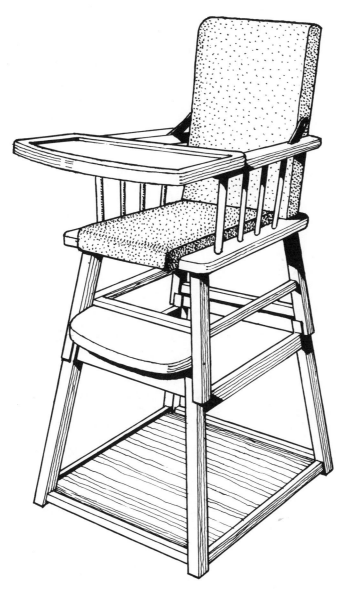

This design has two functions – first, to provide a high chair for a baby when used in conjunction with the lower unit; and second, to act as a small arm chair as the child grows older. For the latter purpose, the lower unit is turned upside down and can be used as a play table.

SEAT

The frame for this consists of three pieces, each 3in by ¾in thick, rebated ½in wide by ⅜in deep, with the back piece tenoned into the side pieces. After assembly, the seat proper rests in these rebates and is further supported at the front by a rail tenoned into the front legs, the top of the rail finishing flush with the top of the rebates; see Figs. 2.1 and 2.3.

The seat consists of ¼in ply to which is glued a 1in thickness of foam rubber covered with a suitable plastic fabric, which should preferably be washable, and this is taken underneath the ply about 1in all round and tacked into place. The seat is fixed into

the rebates by screwing from underneath but this is, of course, not done until the chair framing is completed. Make the ply for the seat about 1/16in smaller all the way round than the rebate size so that you can fit it easily, bearing in mind that the seat projects at the front ½in beyond the side pieces.

LEGS

The legs of the chair are 1¼in by ⅞in and are tenoned into the seat at an angle from both the front and sides. You will therefore have to make full scale elevation drawings (Fig. 2.1) to arrive at the correct angles for the tenon shoulders and mortises. The leg tenons are ⅝in long with shoulder depths of ⅛in all round.

FRAMING RAILS

The lower back and front rails are each stub-tenoned into the legs. These rails are of 1½in by ¾in section, the lower edges being 1½in up from the feet (at the

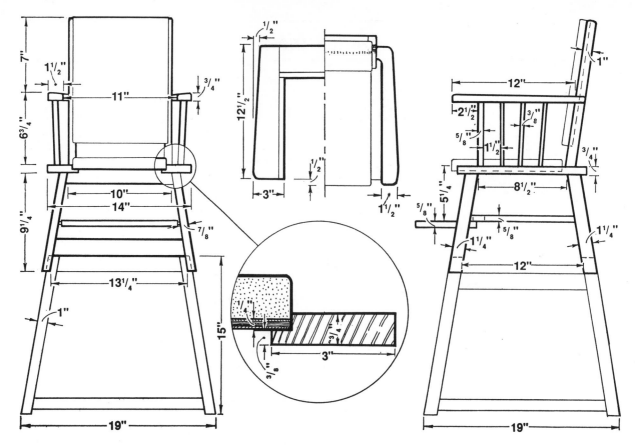

Fig. 2.1. Elevations with principal dimensions. Also, half-plan of seat frame and half-plan of arm in relation to seat.

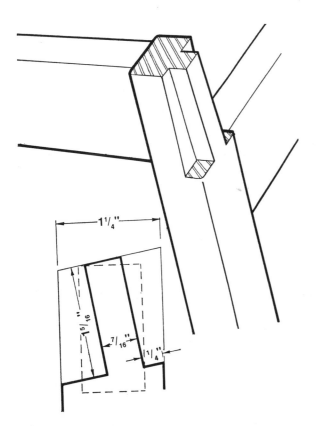

Fig. 2.2. Details of projection on leg of lower unit on to which the slot in the leg of the chair fits. The broken lines of the dimensioned drawing indicate the front rail of the lower unit.

front) to fit against the top rail of the lower unit when the chair is in position on it. Fit hooks and eyes, or the type of fitting-clip used on travel cases, so that there is one on the inside of each of the front and back rails, and these lock the chair to the lower unit.

The two units fit together by means of a slot cut in the bottom of the inside of each four legs; these slide on to similar shaped projections cut in the tops of the legs of the lower unit, see Fig. 2.2. Each slot and projecting piece is 1⁵⁄₁₆in long and they must, of course, be vertical when viewed from the side otherwise the arrangement will not be practicable.

The chair also has side rails of ¾in by ⅝in stub-tenoned into the legs. Between these rails is a single rail set back slightly from the front of the chair to act as a stop for the foot rest when it is in the down position. The foot rest hinges on two ⅜in dowels glued into the ends and fitting in holes drilled in the legs; this allows the foot rest to be folded up out of the way when not in use.

ASSEMBLY

Start with the back and front leg assemblies. You will have to put the foot rest in position at the same time as the front rails are glued in.

The back consists of two pieces with top and bottom rails stub-tenoned into them. The side pieces, which are 1in by ¾in material, are rebated on the front inside edges ⅜in by ⅜in for the purpose of containing the back. This is made from ¼in ply, which is upholstered with 1in foam rubber padding and covered with the same fabric as the seat.

As the side pieces are rebated, the rails are ⅝in thick by 1½in wide. Note from Figs. 2.1 and 2.3 that the top rail tenons are reduced in width by ½in at the top; and the rebates in the side pieces are stopped 2in from the front shoulder of the tenon at the bottom where they join the seat.

ARMS

The shaped arms are dowelled to the side pieces of the back, so drill for the dowels in the arms before shaping them. At the front are two posts of ⅝in

6

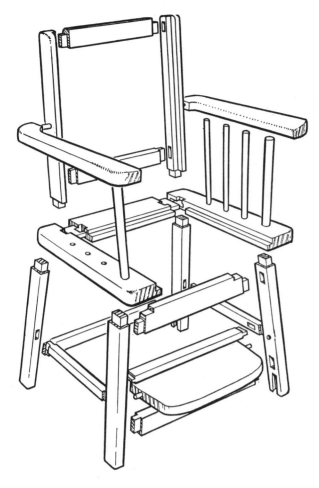

Fig. 2.3. Exploded view of construction.

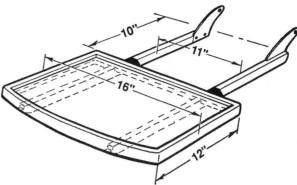

Fig. 2.4. Dimensions of tray: the front may be made straight if preferred.

the tray to be swung out of the way when not required. Although the thickness of the tray arms is given as being ½in (to prevent them from binding when in position between the chair arms), they should be thinned down to finish slightly less than ½in.

FINISH
The upper surfaces of the tray and the table of the lower unit should be covered with a suitable plastic laminate for easy cleaning. If the chair is to be painted you will need to use a lead-free non-toxic paint.

dowel rod which connect the two arms to the seat. These are vertical when viewed from the side, but are set at an angle when seen from the front. The other ⅜in dia rods between the seat and the arms are raked progressively when viewed from the side, but for the sake of simplicity you may prefer to make them all vertical both from the front and the side.

FINAL ASSEMBLY
Assemble the back rails into the side pieces and then attach the arms to the back before putting in the dowels, finally fitting the complete assembly into the seat. Cramp the arms to the side pieces with G-cramps until the adhesive sets. To facilitate this, leave the final shaping of the outsides of the backs of the arms until after assembly.

THE LOWER UNIT
This is quite straightforward, having four posts or legs with top and bottom rails tenoned into them. Look at Fig. 2.1 and you will see that the top side rails are set down 1½in. The bottom rails are of 1in by ¾in wood grooved ¼in by ¼in to accept the ply tray, and the tenons could be mitred at the ends.

THE TRAY
The arms of the tray are ¾in by ½in, and, when the tray is completed, fit between the chair arms. The tray itself is built on the top of the arms so that it rests on the top of the front of the chair arms when in use. Two metal plates are screwed to the back of the tray arms, and a single screw through each of these into the chair back act as hinges which enable

CUTTING LIST

	INCHES			MM		
	L	W	T	L	W	T
Chair						
1 back piece	12½	3⅛	¾	318	80	19
2 side pieces	13	3⅛	¾	330	80	19
4 legs	10½	1⅜	⅞	267	35	22
2 front & back rails	12	1⅝	¾	305	42	19
2 side rails	12½	⅞	⅝	318	22	16
1 cross rail	13½	1⅛	⅝	343	29	16
1 foot rest	11½	6⅛	⅝	292	156	16
1 seat	11	9	¼	279	229	6
2 chair back side pieces	15	1⅛	¾	382	29	19
2 chair back rails	10	1½	⅝	254	38	16
2 arms	13¼	2⅛	¾	337	54	19
2 front posts	7¼	⅝ dia		184	16 dia	
6 dowel rails	7¼	⅜ dia		184	10 dia	
1 chair back	12⅛	9¼	¼	308	235	6
Lower unit						
4 legs	16	1⅜	1	407	35	25
2 top front & back rails	14	1⅝	¾	356	42	19
2 top side rails	15	1⅝	¾	381	42	19
4 bottom rails	19	1⅛	¾	483	29	19
1 table	17½	17½	¼	445	445	6
Tray						
2 arms	22⅛	⅞	½	562	22	12
2 front & back	16¼	¾	½	413	19	12
2 sides	12¼	¾	½	311	19	12
1 top	15⅞	11⅞	¼	405	302	6

Working allowances have been made to lengths and widths; thicknesses are net. The dimensions for the tray front are given here as for a straight piece. If it is required to be curved as in the illustrations, extra thickness will be needed.

CHILD'S ROCKING CHAIR

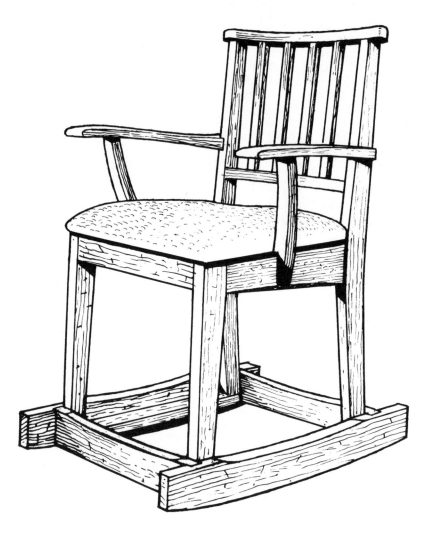

This chair can be used with or without the rockers, which can be removed as one unit. Construction is simple and of the 'flat frame' type. The original design was made from Honduras mahogany, but almost any stable hardwood can be used.

PREPARATION

Try to get 1in sawn material for the legs and keep it as thick as you can.

Make the chair first. Plane up all the material, that for the arms and back legs being prepared with one square edge and thicknessed: the remainder can be prepared to width and thickness. Allow at least 2in waste at each end of the back legs, screw them together at the ends through the waste and then shape them together, marking out the joints on the face edges before you separate them. The front legs, the front and back rails and the side rails are all straight, but chamfered to give a curved appearance on the bottom edge.

JOINTING AND SHAPING

When you mark out the tenons on the side rails, note that they are not in line with the rails, as the chair is wider at the front. To get over this problem, plane a taper at each end of the rail, on opposite sides, and mark from this taper as shown in Fig. 3.1. A word of warning – this taper must be planed very accurately.

Fig. 3.1 also shows the back rail housed and tenoned into the side rails and the front rail tenoned into the front legs. The spandrail and top back rail are mortised and tenoned, the joints being marked out before the curves are shaped. If you keep the timber to ⅞in or more, all the mortises can be 5⁄16in wide – otherwise make them ¼in.

Mark out systematically, keeping all face side marks to the inside and numbering all the joints. The shoulders for the tenons at the top of the back legs and the mortises for the spandrail should be squared from the (front) face edges of the legs (see Fig. 3.1), so that the shoulders on the spars are all square. The arm supports are housed and screwed and glued into the side rails for easy assembly, the chair being glued up and the arms fitted last of all.

Shape the profiles of the arms together, as you did with the back legs. Plane the taper (B) Fig. 3.2 from which to gauge the tenon. Don't shape the supports

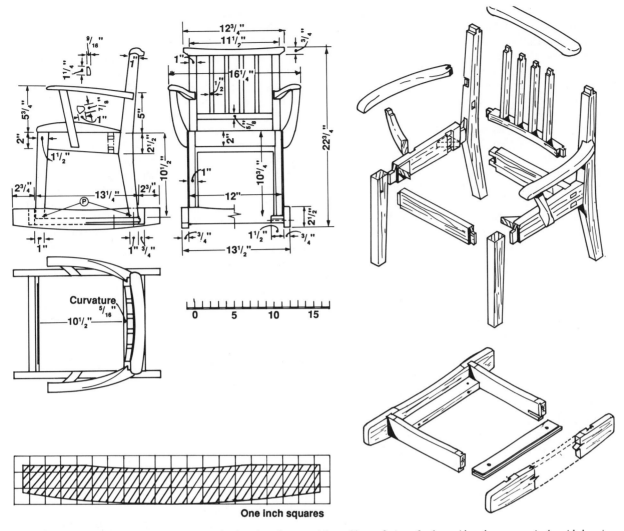

Fig. 3.1. Elevations and plan. Points P on side elevation show position of brass fittings for legs. Also shown: one inch-grid drawing of rocker and (right) exploded views of construction.

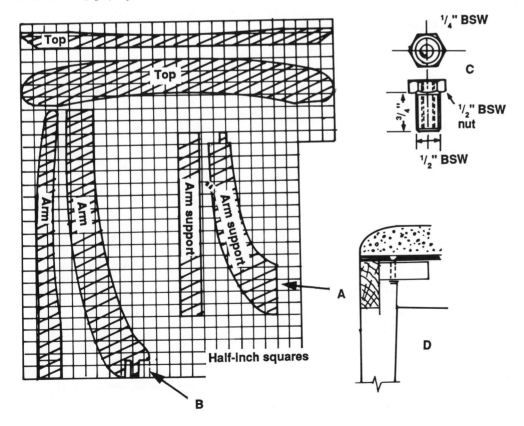

Fig. 3.2. Half-inch grid details of top rail, arm, and arm support. C shows sizes of brass fittings for legs; and D, detail of bolting ply seat through corner blocks.

9

yet, but plane the surfaces (A) Fig. 3.2 to mate with the side rails at the correct angle. Mark out the housings on the side rails for the arm supports.

Next, cut all joints, including those between the arms and the legs, noting that each arm goes square into its leg. To mark out the joint between the arm and support, cramp the side rail and the back and front legs together.

Do each side separately – there is no need to assemble the complete chair. Get the bevel at the top by fitting the arm into the leg and cramping the support into its housing so that the top end just touches the arm. Set a bevel gauge to get the shoulder angle, and at the same time mark the extremes of the mortise under the arm. Mark out the bevelled shoulders for the tenon from the face side and edge of the support. Gauge the tenon from a piece of scrap wood which can be cramped or screwed against the sloping face (A) of the support, Fig. 3.2.

Gauge the mortise under the arm from the edge of a piece of wood cramped flat on top of the arm, and lined up with the tenon at the end. When you are cutting the mortise, remember that it is at an angle. Once the joints are cut, the arms and their supports can be shaped. Be careful near the mortises on the arms – it would be all too easy to cut into the mortise here, and impossible to hide the mistake.

ASSEMBLY

Now clean up the inside surfaces and assemble the chair. Glue and cramp the sides together first, separately that is, the side rails and the front and back legs. Clean up the inside of these sub-assemblies when the adhesive has set, and glue and cramp them together by means of the front and back rails and the spandrail. Before fitting the spars and the top back rail, glue and cramp the arms in. Screw the supports in dry (without adhesive) for a test fit and then take them apart. Glue the joints at the end of each arm and assemble; then fit the supports, screwing and gluing them to the side rails.

Fit a notched piece of wood over the arms so that they will not spread, and cramp down to the side rails. Two more cramps will be needed to pull the arms back into the back leg; do this with the top back rail loosely in position. Fit the spars and top back rail last of all and not until the adhesive on the arms has set.

Now screw and glue angle blocks into the corners of the chair, as shown, 1/8in below the top of the seat rails.

SEAT

The upholstered seat was made by fixing a pad of plastic foam, cut to shape, to a piece of 6mm plywood and covering it with uncut moquette, using a fabric adhesive.

The seat is fixed down with four small countersunk bolts through the corner blocks. Extra nuts keep them in place, and the thickness of these nuts is the reason for dropping the corner blocks 1/8in. Put the bolts through the ply before you cover the seat!

THE ROCKER

This consists of a separate frame, jointed with stopped dovetail housings, only one side of each housing being dovetailed. The chair rests on supports glued and screwed to the curved rocker sides, and tongued into the cross rails of the assembly. As the chair is wider at the front, the front measurement is taken as the inside dimension of the rocker assembly; the difference at the back can be made up with glued blocks. The curve on the sides of the rocker must not be too great, otherwise a child could trap his feet under it or tip the chair over backwards.

Note that, although the grooves in the cross rails for the tongues on the ends of the chair supports are full width, the tongues on the supports are cut short. When you glue up the rocker, the supports are glued into the cross rails first. As the end tongues are cut short, the supports can be pulled inwards a little. The faces of the supports mating with the sides of the rocker are glued, the cross rail joints are glued and the two cross rails pushed home. Then the supports can be pushed outwards into position and screwed to the sides, and cramps put over the cross rails. Unless you give the supports this small sideways movement, you'll find it impossible to assemble the frame.

Finally, clean up and glasspaper the sub-assembly.

FIXING AND FINISHING

To fasten the chair to the rocker, four 1in lengths of 1/2in brass studding are required. Four thin brass nuts are soft-soldered to one end of each, as shown in Fig. 3.2, and each one is then drilled and tapped 1/4in.

The chair legs are bored 7/16in for about 1 1/2in and a 1/2in taper tap screwed in. Do this gently to avoid reaming out a 1/2in hole; the tapped brass bushes are then smeared with an epoxy resin adhesive and screwed into the legs. Four 1 1/2in by 1/4in dia roundhead screws through the supports in the rockers will hold them to the chair.

Alternatively, bolt the legs of the chair through the rocker sides with wing nuts.

The chair was finished with two coats of teak oil, and took about two weekends to complete, for very little cost.

CUTTING LIST

	INCHES			MM		
	L	W	T	L	W	T
2 back legs	24	2½	15/16	610	64	24
2 front legs	12	1¾	15/16	305	45	24
2 side rails	12	2¾	¾	305	70	19
1 front rail	12	2¼	¾	305	58	19
1 back rail	11½	2¾	¾	292	70	19
2 arms from one piece	15	3¾	1	381	95	25
2 arm supports from one piece	11	3	⅞	279	76	22
1 top back rail	14	2	¾	356	51	19
1 spandrail	12	1½	¾	305	38	19
1 seat	12½	11½	¼	318	292	6
4 spars	8½	¾	½	216	19	12
2 rocker sides	19¼	2¾	⅞	489	70	22
2 rocker chair supports	13¾	1¾	¾	349	45	19
2 rocker cross rails	13	2¼	¾	330	58	19
4 corner blocks from 1 piece	12	2	⅞	305	51	22

Working allowances have been made to lengths and widths; thicknesses are net.

WINDSOR-STYLE CHILD'S HIGH CHAIR

Suitable for a child of from one and a half to four years of age, this chair is the correct height to suit a normal dining table. It is a useful lesson in making chairs of the Windsor type, and also gives good practice in 'between-centres' turning.

LEGS
Begin by turning these. Try to get a nice flowing curve from the major to the minor diameters, locating the major where indicated on the drawing.

SEAT
Select a piece of sound timber for this, without any splits or shakes. You could use plywood, which would probably be stronger but would not have such a good appearance when finished. Set the seat out as shown; cut the outline to shape and curve the edges.

DRILLING THE SEAT
The holes for the legs can most conveniently be

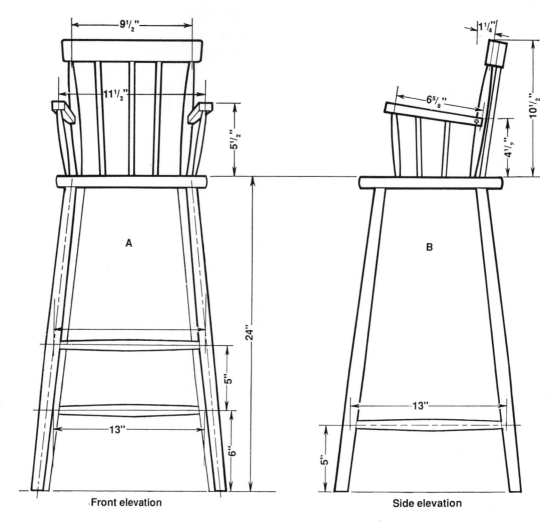

Fig. 4.1. Front and side elevations.

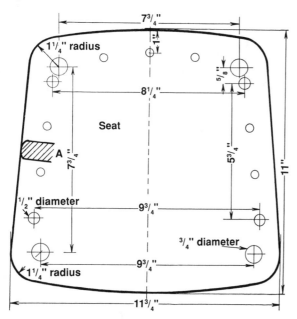

Fig. 4.2. Details of seat and boring.

drilled on a pillar drill with a canting table. Figs. 4.2 and 4.5 show how this can be done. Set the table over to about 12½ degrees, remembering that the line of cant is diagonal from corner to corner of the seat – this gives the correct splay of the legs in both planes. These holes should be drilled from the underside of the seat, and the seat itself is clamped to the machine table with a waste piece of wood beneath to get a clean breakthrough on the holes. This will give a

better finish to the hole on the upper side than if you drill from the top.

The holes for the back uprights and the arm stumps are drilled from the upper side with the cant angle reduced to about 8 degrees, and when drilling these holes you should position the seat diagonally on the table as before. The holes for the intermediate spindles can be left until the top work is ready for assembly.

DRILLING THE LEGS

Fig. 4.4 shows how to drill the legs for the stretchers. The angle of the table is as for the leg holes in the seat, namely 12½ degrees, and the leg rests in a vee trough which is cramped to the table. When setting out the holes for the stretchers, bear in mind that they are handed and so, when drilled, must form two pairs. Attaching the pin of the leg to the lathe carrier is an easy way of indexing it to get the 90 degree turn from the first to the second hole in each leg, and you can do this by very carefully sighting the carrier horizontally for the first hole and vertically for the second.

STRETCHERS

Dowelling of ⅝in dia can be used for these. If your lathe has a hollow mandrel of ⅝in bore or more, they can best be done in a self-centering chuck, but if the mandrel is not hollow they will have to be turned between centres. In this case, they could be turned out of ¾in stuff and given a fully shaped curve from end to end; with care in centering, it should be possible to hold the major diameter up to ¹¹⁄₁₆in.

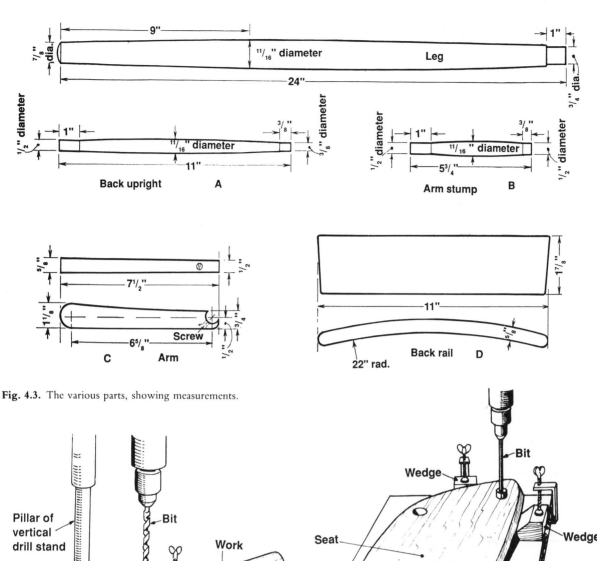

Fig. 4.3. The various parts, showing measurements.

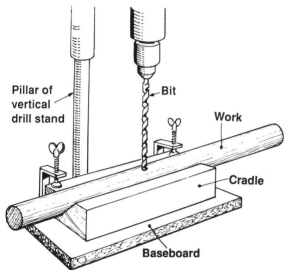

Fig. 4.4. Boring a leg for a stretcher.

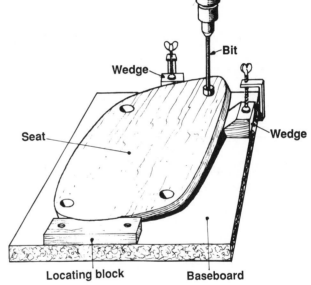

Fig. 4.5. Boring a seat.

PART ASSEMBLY

Before assembling and glueing up the lower part of the chair, cut the saw kerfs in the pins for wedging. Take care that these are positioned in relation to the stretcher holes so that the line of the wedge is at right angles to the grain of the seat, as this will help to prevent any likelihood of splitting the seat when driving in the wedges. After assembly and before the adhesive sets check the frame for symmetry, glue and insert the wedges, and put the sub-assembly aside for the adhesive to set.

BACK AND ARMS

The main back uprights and arm stumps are shaped as shown in Fig. 4.3. You can shape the top back rail by hand with first a bow saw, followed by spoke-shaving, scraping, and finishing with glasspaper. An easier way is to use a bandsaw, if you have one, and

if the rail is sawn carefully it can be speedily finished on a disc and belt sander. Insert the back uprights and arm stumps dry (unglued) to act as guides for drilling the blind holes in the seat for the intermediate uprights in the back and arms. After fitting, the rear ends of the arms are fixed to the back uprights with ¾in raised head brass screws, but it is a good idea to insert steel screws temporarily which are replaced by the brass ones for final assembly.

Spend some time in getting a pleasing shape to the arms as it can add much to the final appearance.

FINAL ASSEMBLY

First, make a trial assembly of the whole of the top part dry (unglued) to make sure that everything will come together satisfactorily before finally glueing up. The arm stumps and back uprights are wedged from underneath and the upper ends pegged with

⅛in dowels through the arms and back rail respectively.

FINISHING

After a final clean up with glasspaper, the chair can be finished with three coats of polyurethane lacquer. The first coat can be thinned with 10% white spirit (mineral spirits) and, when dry, this can be glasspapered lightly to remove dust nibs. The second coat should be well rubbed down and, again, all dust nibs removed before applying the final coat – this should be applied in as dust-free an atmosphere as possible. The final coat can be left off-the-brush, or if you prefer a satin finish you can rub it down with steel wool and wax it; this type of finish should well resist the kind of wear to which the chair will be subjected.

CUTTING LIST

	INCHES			MM		
	L	W	T	L	W	T
4 legs	24½	1¼ dia		622	32 dia	
2 back uprights	11½	¾ dia		292	19 dia	
2 arm stumps	6	¾ dia		153	19 dia	
2 arms	7¾	1¼	⅝	197	32	16
1 back rail	11½	2	1½	292	51	38
1 seat	12	11½	¾	305	292	19
4 leg stretchers	13	⅝ dia		330	16 dia	
3 back intermediate uprights	11	⅜ dia		279	10 dia	
2 arm intermediate uprights	6	⅜ dia		153	10 dia	
2 arm intermediate uprights	5½	⅜ dia		140	10 dia	

Working allowances have been made to lengths and widths; thicknesses are net.

NESTING CHAIRS FOR THE NURSERY

These strong chairs are designed for rough use in a small nursery of several children. The sizes given will suit a very young child, but for older children, they will need to be increased in proportion. Two of the chairs stacked can be used to make a high chair for a child at a meal table. By drilling a series of holes, you can make the height of the chair seat adjustable, and another advantage is that the chairs can be dismantled for packing purposes.

Choose a good quality straight and close-grained hardwood, as this will look attractive if polished or waxed a natural colour. If you wish, the chair seat can be bent plywood instead of the slats as shown, and the table top covered with an easily cleaned and heatproof plastic laminate.

GENERAL CONSTRUCTION

Most of the timber is 1in nominal thickness which finishes ⅞in thick after being planed and glass-papered. When you prepare the legs (C) they should be left long, and they need to be stop-grooved for the side rails (D) which are tongued to the legs. Set out the side framing full size on a piece of plywood or stout paper to the dimensions shown in the side elevation in Fig. 5.1 as this will give the angle for the shoulders.

Glue together and trim off the tops and bottoms of the legs. Shape and round off the edges of the arms (E); screw them down to the top edges of the side frames, the screw-heads being recessed and the holes pelleted.

SEAT

The seat frame is through-tenoned and dovetailed together, the top edges of the side rails being shaped as in Fig. 5.1; screw the slats to the frame with countersunk head screws. Do this carefully to prevent splitting the slats and to avoid oversunk screw heads. If you use plywood instead of slats, screw it down with roundhead brass or nickel-plated screws.

BACK

The uprights are connected by the two rails, (A) and (B). Shape the top rail (A) to the bent plywood (see plan, Fig. 5.1), and notch it to the uprights (H) and screw   in place, Fig. 5.2. The bottom rail is stub-tenoned to the uprights, and the latter should be eased away as shown in Fig. 5.1 to the bend of the plywood back. This back is bent and screwed to the framing with raised head brass or nickel-plated screws.

ASSEMBLY

Now drill ¼in dia holes in the side framing, Fig. 5.1, and through the side rails of the seat frame; these rails should be given a slight slope towards the back as in the side elevation, Fig. 5.1. Use four round-head coach bolts 2½in long by ¼ diameter to bolt the sides and the seat together, with wing nuts and washers under the nuts. You can attach the back to the seat

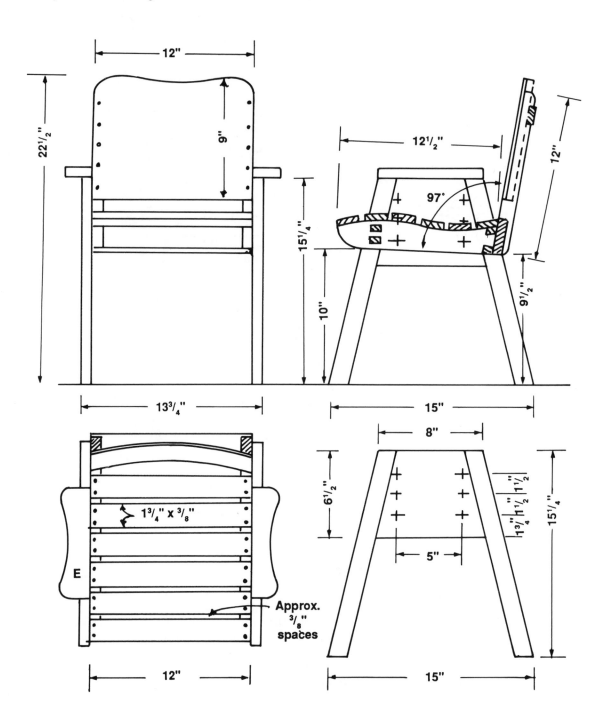

Fig. 5.1. Front and side elevations, and plan; with dimensions.

16

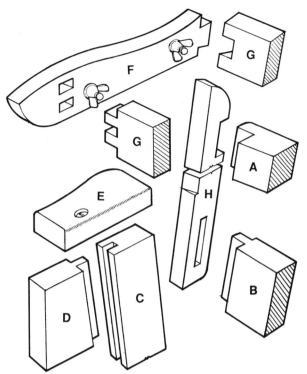

Fig. 5.2. Types of joints used.

on the way by drilling through the bottom back rail and the back seat rails. Screw the nuts up tight before use. The seats can be provided with squab cushions tied to the back uprights if you wish.

CUTTING LIST

	INCHES			MM		
	L	W	T	L	W	T
Part						
A 1 back rail	12½	1¾	1¼	318	45	32
B 1 back rail	12	3	⅞	305	76	22
C 4 legs	16½	1⅝	⅞	419	42	22
D 2 side rails	9½	6¾	⅞	242	172	22
E 2 arms	8½	2½	⅞	216	64	22
F 2 pieces for seat	13	2½	⅞	330	64	22
G 2 pieces for seat	12½	2½	⅞	318	64	22
H 2 back uprights	12½	1½	⅞	318	38	22
J 6 seat slats	12½	2	⅜	318	51	10
K 1 back panel	9½	13	¼	242	330	6

Working allowances have been made to lengths and widths; thicknesses are net. Note: in part K, the longer dimension indicates the grain direction.

MODULAR STACKING CHAIR UNITS

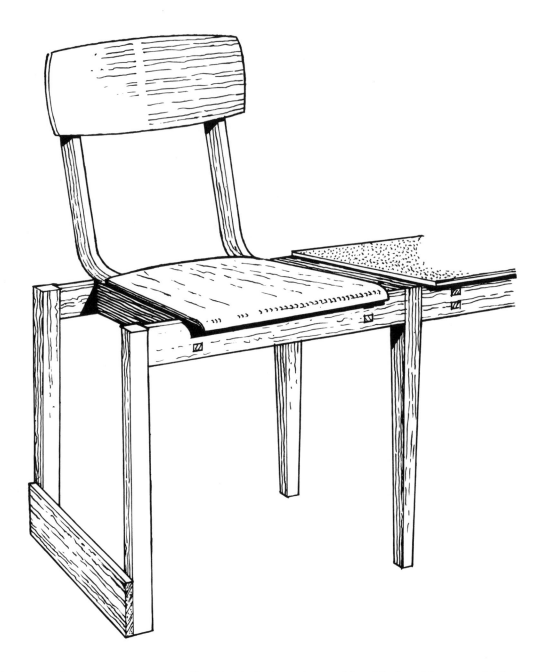

Such designs as there are on the market for this kind of seating furniture are usually single chairs that tend to be time and energy consuming to move and stack, and often the stacking is untidy and precarious. The design shown here consists of a unit of two seats with a table interposed built to a modular size, and is ideally suited for use in schools, meeting halls, waiting rooms and similar places.

THE MODULE
This governs the size and number of seats dend is determined by the several factors of weight, the length of the unit in relation to the place where it is to be used, and the number which can easily and safely be stacked. A useful feature is that the seats are interchangeable with the table tops, which makes the design more versatile.

To avoid confusion all the following instructions and requirements relate to a *single* unit, and, unless otherwise stated, the timber is good quality close-grained hardwood.

CONSTRUCTION OF THE UNDERFRAME
Start by preparing the two side rails, and then the eight legs. Note that the four inside legs are tapered from 1¼in to 1in as shown in Fig. 6.1. The four end ones should be marked out and cut for haunched mortise and tenon joints, while the remaining four have tee-bridle joints, see Figs. 6.1 and 6.2.

Next, prepare the front and back rails to match the

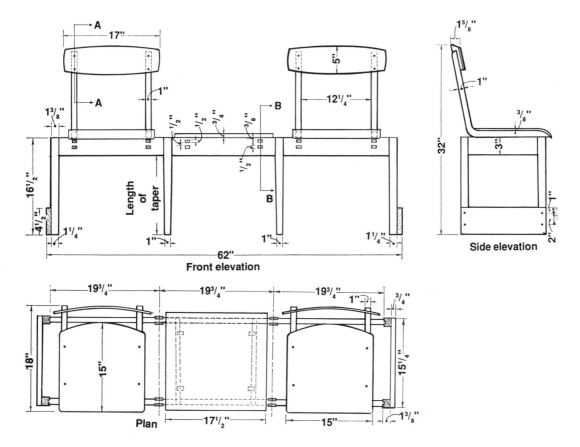

Fig. 6.1. Front and side elevations, with plan.

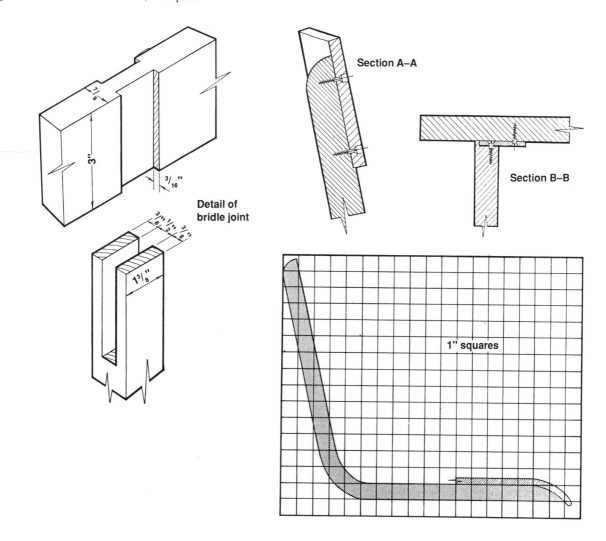

Fig. 6.2. Bridle joint, fixing of back and table top. Also, squared-off drawing of seat and back support.

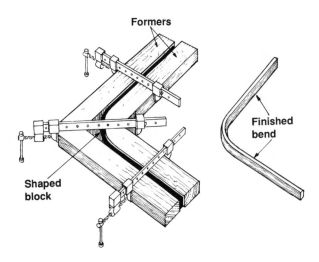

Formers

Finished bend

Shaped block

Fig. 6.3. Arrangement of formers for the supports.

joints cut on the legs, that is, a haunched tenon at each end and the two bridle joints on each rail (Figs. 6.1 and 6.2). Follow this by preparing the six cross rails, which have twin stub tenons at each end fitting into through mortises on the front and back rails; see Fig. 6.1. These rails, of course, locate and support the seat (or table top).

Now clean up the parts and glue and assemble them, wiping away any excess adhesive with a damp cloth. To facilitate stacking, a rail is screwed to the outside of the end legs which provides a level surface on which the units can stack. It also prevents the chairs from tipping forwards when stacked.

SEATS AND SUPPORTS

Two pieces of ¼in veneered plywood are used for the laminations of the seat backs and seats. Arrange the grain of the exterior veneers to run across the seats in order to achieve the bend on the leading edge.

The size of the plywood used for the seat is 16in square, and for the back rest 18in by 6in; both sizes allow a surplus for subsequent cleaning up and shaping.

The back seat supports are laminated, and to do this you will need to make up three simple formers from softwood. Fig. 6.2 (which is squared off into half inch squares) shows the profile, and the cramped up formers are illustrated in Fig. 6.3.

Sixteen mahogany veneers (any good hardwood veneers would be equally suitable), each 30in long by 1¼in wide, are needed for each support. The con-

struction for each one is rather a lengthy affair, and you will find it a good idea to use a thin mixture of a PVA adhesive, diluted with water as recommended by the manufacturer, which slows down the setting time – lightly dampening the veneers is also advantageous. Fig. 6.3 shows the cramping up of the formers.

ASSEMBLY

Now shape the seat and back supports to suit the curvature of the seat, and drill and screw them on to the cross rails of the underframe, using three 2in countersunk head screws per rail (Fig. 6.2). Next, screw the backs and seats to the supports; the screws need to be sunk ¼in to accommodate a hardwood dowel plug or pellet, (Fig. 6.2).

TABLE TOP

This can be made from a piece of veneered or plastic laminate-faced plywood 16in square by ¾in thick, with the edges veneered or plastic-lipped. It is fitted to the cross rails by means of four table plates although, if it is to be removed frequently, a suitable knock-down fitting could be used instead.

FINISH

The chairs can be finished with three coats of clear cellulose lacquer, cutting down each coat lightly with steel wool to attain a matt finish which will stand up to hard wear and which can be easily wiped clean.

CUTTING LIST

	INCHES			*MM*		
	L	W	T	L	W	T
8 legs	17	1½	1¼	432	38	32
2 rails	59¾	3¼	⅞	1517	83	22
6 cross rails	15¾	3¼	⅞	400	83	22
2 end rails	15¾	4¾	⅞	400	121	22
96 laminations for 6 supports	30	1½	1.5mm	762	38	1.5
6 seats, ply	16	16	¼	407	407	6
6 backs, ply	18	6	¼	457	153	6
1 table top, ply (optional)	18	16¾	¼	457	425	6

Working allowances have been made to lengths and widths; thicknesses are net.

SWIVEL CHAIR

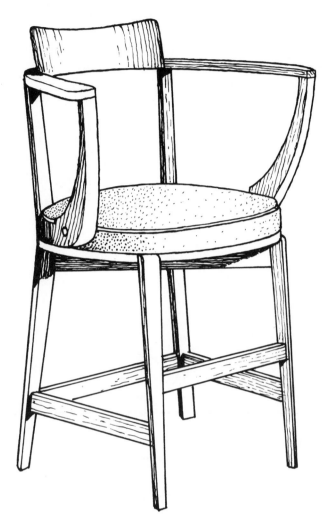

Although at first glance this swivel chair may appear complicated, it is not, but it does call for accurate work throughout and a good quality hardwood should be used. Walnut is the chief wood used but other hardwoods are equally suitable. The chair was designed to go with a small desk and for this reason is less bulky than the usual type of square swivel chair.

DRAWINGS

Begin by making a full-size plan and drawing out the two elevations shown in Fig. 7.2. The plan shows the legs joined by diagonal rails slot-dovetailed down into them. The elevation obtained when looking in the direction of the arrow X shows the true length and shape of the legs, the rail and the back support which is really a continuation of the back leg. The height dimensions in the auxiliary elevations are the same as in the front and side elevations in Fig. 7.1.

PREPARATION

Prepare the four legs to length and shape them by tapering as shown in the drawings. Taper the front legs on three sides to finish ¾in square at floor level as indicated by the dotted lines in Fig. 7.3, while the

back legs are tapered on one side only to finish 1¼in by ¾in at floor level. Cut the diagonal rails to length and slot-dovetail them to the legs, putting an identification mark on each joint as it is fitted. The rails are joined to each other by a cross-halving joint.

The plan, Fig. 7.2, shows how the lower rails are joined to the legs. Saw the ends of the rails square and fit them to the legs by means of two dowels in each joint. You can find the exact length of the rails by drawing them in on the full size plan in Fig. 7.2.

First draw the elevation obtained by viewing in the direction of the arrow Y and project from it the position of the rail in plan. The tricky part of the work is cutting the notches in the legs to accommodate the rails. After you have marked the position of the rails on the legs, temporarily assemble them. A try square resting on the floor with its blade against each leg in turn will give the vertical lines marking the depth of the notches, as indicated in Fig. 7.3. You can then cut the notches and try each rail separately for fit.

PRE-ASSEMBLY WORK

You can now assemble all the rails to check for accurate fitting all round and for any adjustments

Fig. 7.1. Front and side elevations, with sections.

which need to be made. Mark out the holes for the dowels accurately by using a template, and then carefully bore the holes and prepare the dowels.

The corners of all the legs are either chamfered or rounded, as shown in Fig. 7.3, to give a lighter appearance. You can now clean up the legs and rails and polish them ready for final assembly. Locate any joint identification marks where they will not be cleaned off, as they are necessary to ensure that the joints are assembled correctly.

ASSEMBLY

This is done in two stages. First, glue the front and back rails to each pair of legs, then cramp them up and put them aside for the glue to set. Take care that the legs and rail retain the correct shape – to ensure this, use a strip of waste wood (A) at the top of the legs as indicated in Fig. 7.4, and then check the diagonals to see they are equal.

Shape some waste pieces of wood (B) to fit the legs and to act as cramping blocks. When the glue has set, glue and cramp the remaining two lower rails in place, and also drop in and glue the two diagonal rails into the dovetail slots.

SEAT

Make the circular base and seat next. The base consists of four pieces dowelled together or joined by plywood tongues as indicated in the plan, Fig. 7.2. The seat is of similar construction, except that eight pieces are used as shown in Fig. 7.6. Insert a piece of cardboard between the base and the seat frames, and screw both together temporarily so that the thin facing strip (rim) can be bent and glued all round; bearing in mind that the joint between the ends of the strip when bent round should come where it will be hidden by a leg. The rim projects ³/₁₆in or so to hide the edge of the upholstery. Pieces (A) and (B) are joined to each other by a cross-halving joint.

Bend the strip round and cramp it up to try for fit

before applying the glue. Cramp it well to make sure it fits closely and forms a true circle. When the glue has set, remove the cramps and separate the seat from the base by sawing through the facing strip all round but, before doing this, clean the whole thing up. Fix the base in place by glueing and screwing it to the diagonal rails, with a shallow housing to the projection on the legs.

BACK

This consists of a semi-circular portion and two straight parts which act as arm rests. Make the whole shape of strips of 3mm plywood (with a facing strip each side) which need to be bent and glued round a former of the kind indicated in Fig. 7.7. Glue the strips to each other while flat and hold them at the centre by panel pins driven through; finally, glue on the facing strips which are held at the centre with fine panel pins.

Now cramp the laminate to the centre of the former. Use a spare strip of plywood or a thin flexible steel strap (if you have one) on the outer surface to take the pressure of the G-cramps. Insert strips of paper between the laminate and the former, and between the laminate and the outer strip to prevent sticking should any glue find its way through. Working from the centre, bend and cramp the complete laminate to the former. When the glue has set, remove the cramps and glue the additional tapered pieces to the outside to finish the shape of the arms. Now proceed to veneer the upper and lower surfaces, and cut the mortises to take the back uprights and the arm supports.

ARM SUPPORTS

Mark these out after making a cardboard template; then cut them out to the initial shape, the final shape being achieved by rounding off the corners. Glue and screw the supports in place, noting that they are housed into the seat rim; counterbore the hole for the

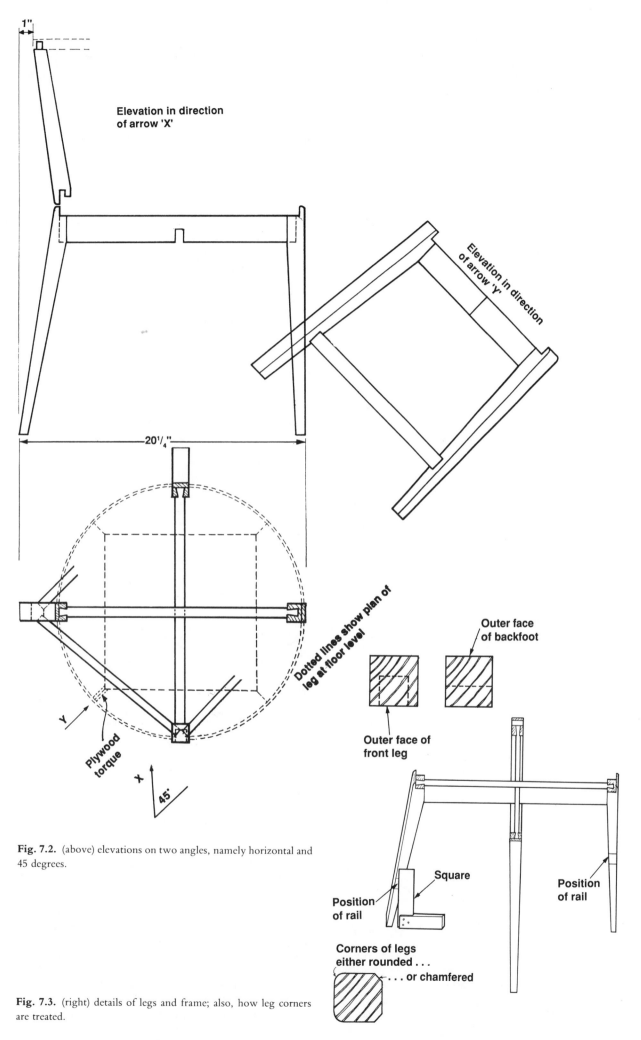

Elevation in direction of arrow 'X'

1"

Elevation in direction of arrow 'y'

20¹/₄"

Dotted lines show plan of leg at floor level

Y

Plywood torque

X

45°

Fig. 7.2. (above) elevations on two angles, namely horizontal and 45 degrees.

Outer face of backfoot

Outer face of front leg

Square

Position of rail

Position of rail

Corners of legs either rounded . . .

. . . or chamfered

Fig. 7.3. (right) details of legs and frame; also, how leg corners are treated.

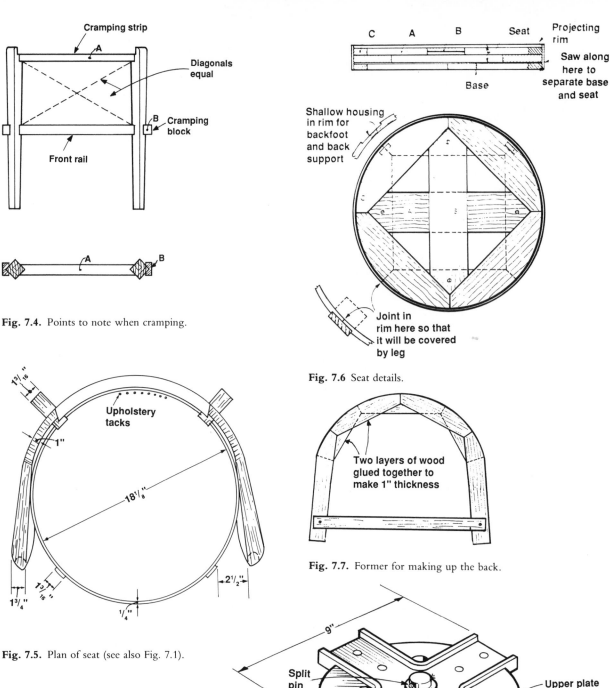

Fig. 7.4. Points to note when cramping.

Fig. 7.6 Seat details.

Fig. 7.5. Plan of seat (see also Fig. 7.1).

Fig. 7.7. Former for making up the back.

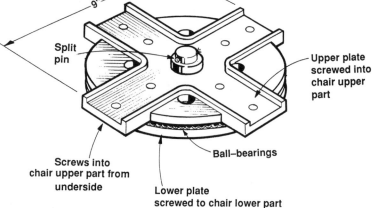

Fig. 7.8. Revolving mechanism.

screw so that a wood pellet can be glued in afterwards. These pellets are small decorative features and can be of a contrasting wood and protrude sufficiently to allow them to be rounded off.

UPHOLSTERY

Clean up and polish the seat and back portion of the chair before starting the upholstery.

This simply consists of a circular piece of polyether foam laid in place and stuck down with an upholstery adhesive. Cover it with a circular piece of fabric or leather which can be held in place with tacks; if you tap in dome-headed upholstery nails so that their

heads cover the tacks it will make the job look professional. Make the back rest by building up laminations round a former in the same way as you did for the back/arms laminate, and then screw it in place.

The revolving mechanism is screwed to the seat and to the diagonal rails of the chair. It is shown in Fig. 7.8 and consists of two plates which revolve on

24

a ball-race fixed between them; the lower circular plate passes through the upper one and is held there by a split pin. So that the seat will lock in the position shown in the elevations in Fig 7.1, fix a circular track of brass or other suitable metal to the base; the track should have two holes to engage ball catches. The latter can be fixed underneath the seat to engage with the holes in the track. Use an epoxy adhesive for bonding the track which should be let in flush with the surface of the base.

CUTTING LIST

	INCHES			MM		
	L	W	T	L	W	T
Top unit						
4 legs	17	1½	1¼	430	38	32
2 top rails	17¾	2	¾	451	51	19
4 bottom rails	13¾	1⅜	⅝	350	35	16

CUTTING LIST (continued)

	INCHES			MM		
	L	W	T	L	W	T
4 base rails	12¾	3⅝	⅝	324	92	16
Bottom unit						
8 seat rails	12¾	3⅝	⅝	324	92	16
2 seat rails	15¾	3⅝	⅝	400	92	16
1 rim	56	2½	3/16	1422	63	5
2 back supports	11⅞	1½	1¼	302	38	32
2 arm supports from	12¾	3¼	1¼	324	83	32
6 laminations, ply,						
for back/arms	43½	1¼	⅛	1105	32	3
2 face laminations	43½	1¼	⅛	1105	32	3
4 back rest						
laminations	15¾	1¾	⅛	400	45	3

Working allowances have been made to lengths and widths; thicknesses are net.

MINI FOLDING CHAIR

Young children love to have something of their own that is different and this chair will bring hours of enjoyment to the lucky owner.

GENERAL CONSTRUCTION

This requires accuracy and patience because you must constantly check that the opening and closing action is correct while you are making the legs, rails, and stays. The distances between centres of the holes and the shoulder distances of the rails are critical for smooth operation.

You can vary the dimensions, of course; I simply followed my own idea of what seemed aesthetically and functionally right. A design drawing alone will not be enough on its own to solve all the problems, and you will almost certainly have to use some trial and error methods – tedious, but not difficult.

As the chair will probably spend much of its time out of doors, choose a hardwood that will stand up

to the weather and to plenty of misuse! All fastenings, stays, etc should be either galvanised or non-ferrous metal.

SEAT

Fig. 8.1 shows the side elevation when open and Fig. 8.2 the seat details. Make the seat unit first, because this decides the widths of the frames, and also the all-important hole positions. For the chair to fold properly, the 7/16in spigots turned on the ends of the 5/8in front and rear seat frame dowels should turn freely in the side rails (Fig. 8.2).

Fig. 8.3 shows the profile of the seat side rails, which have a groove in them for the seat slats. Mark out the centres for the 7/16in spigot pivot holes at the front and back, and the 1/2in stiffener dowel (Fig. 8.2), then cut the groove – a router and guide template is best for this. The top edge of the groove must not be more than 1/8in below the rail top. A

26

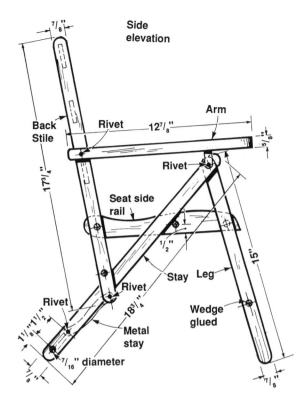

Fig. 8.1. Side elevation when open, with dimensions.

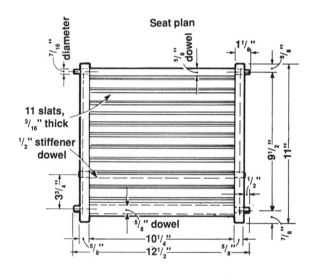

Fig. 8.2. Plan of seat, with dimensions.

³⁄₁₆in or ¼in dia cutter with a bottom cut will be fine, but if you use a ¼in, make sure the front holes are positioned so that the seat frame dowels (⅝in diameter, 10¼in between shoulders) will not foul the front slat.

When assembled, the front edge of the seat should fall away smoothly, the seat frame dowel and the slat both on a radius. If you don't have a router, you can use a drill stand, cutting the groove with a ³⁄₁₆in engineers' drill. Grind the end square, then form cutting wings by grinding the bevels to make a bottom cut. Draw the outline accurately on the seat rails, then follow that freehand, moving the work below the drill, and making light cuts at increasing depths. Drill ⅜in holes at either end of the groove first.

Whichever way you do it, it's best to cut the groove first in oversize square-ended pieces with the profile drawn out on the inner faces, then cut them to shape afterwards. This makes routing with template and clamps easier – but be careful not to make two lefts or two rights! Also make sure you check for possible groove/hole fouling. Drill the holes after you have cut the groove – all holes, of course, should be done on a drill stand to be certain that they are vertical.

Measure the linear length of the curving groove by bending a thin lath or a piece of wire along it, and decide on your slat width and hence the number required. Keep them quite narrow for a bit of flexibility; eleven slats seems about right.

Cut them slightly oversize and trim them to fit, bevelling the top edges to give a slight vee-groove effect. Assemble the frame sides, seat frame dowels, stiffener, and slats dry (without glue); check that everything is square, then take the assembly apart and glasspaper everything carefully. Make a cut in the ends of the ½in stiffener for wedges, and wax the pivot spigots for noise-free operation; then glue up the seat, wedging the stiffener ends.

BACK AND ARMS

You will find from Fig. 8.4 that 11¾in is given as the shoulder length for the 15in by ⅝in dowel that effectively decides the width of the frame; before you turn the ⁷⁄₁₆in spigots with that shoulder length, check that it will allow the seat to fold inside. The extra outside lengths bear on the back stays when the chair is folded out. If 11¾in is not right, give it a bit more (or less) and remember that the adjustment will also affect the length of the back slats. These are 1½in by ³⁄₁₆in (being quite thin for some resiliency) with

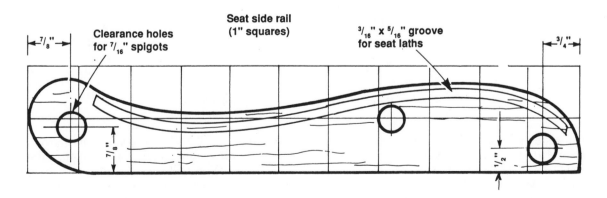

Fig. 8.3. One-inch grid drawing of seat side rail.

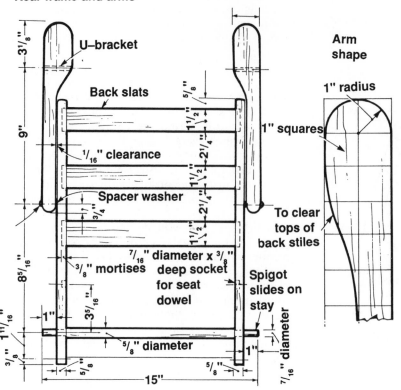

Fig. 8.4. Rear frame and arms; also shape of arm.

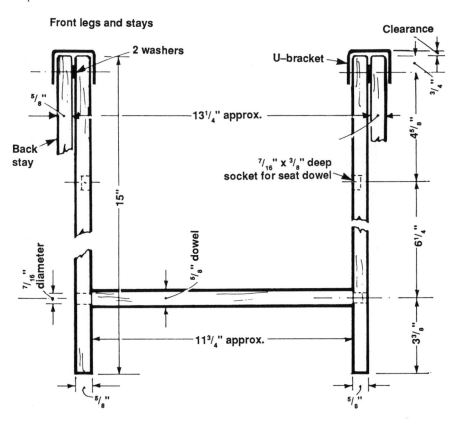

Fig. 8.5. Details of front legs and stays, with dimensions.

all their edges radiused; choose pieces with a nice grain pattern for these as well as for the arms and the seat slats. The back slats sit in mortises 1½in by ³⁄₁₆in, ⅜in deep.

The profile of the shaped front part of the arms is shown in Fig. 8.4. Cut it out – 2in goes to 1in – but leave it oversize so you can do the final shaping after a test assembly. The shaped parts should clear the tops of the back upstands when the chair is folded up, of course. You will have to use the rivets loose in their holes for this and other similar test assemblies. Assemble and glue the back frame together with the spigots of the back seat frame dowel sitting in their sockets in the upstands. Rivet the arms but,

28

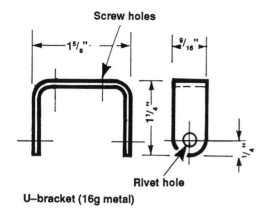

Screw holes

1⁵/₈"

⁹/₁₆"

1¹/₄"

Rivet hole

¹/₄"

U–bracket (16g metal)

Fig. 8.6. Detail of U-bracket.

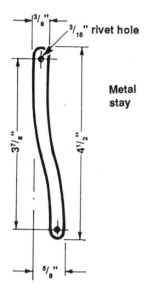

³/₈"

³/₁₆" rivet hole

Metal stay

3⁷/₈"

4¹/₂"

⁵/₈"

Fig. 8.7. Metal stay.

most importantly, do not close the rivets. Glue and pin the spigots of the back seat frame dowels in the upstands, making sure they turn easily in the seat frame itself. Make the U brackets (Fig. 8.6), and fix them to the arms as shown in Figs. 8.4 and 8.5.

FRONT LEGS AND BACK STAYS

Study Fig. 8.5 to see how the front legs and back stay arrangement work. Since you have the back frame assembled with the seat attached by its back seat frame dowels, you can check the distance between centres of the front seat frame dowel and the top U bracket pivot. It is shown as 4⅝in; mark it as such and do a dry test to see that it all works before you drill. Do another dry assembly, then wedge-glue the bottom ⅝in dowel, approximately 11¾in between

the shoulders of the turned ⁷/₁₆in spigots, and glue and pin the front seat frame dowel spigots in their holes. Again, be careful that the spigots themselves turn freely in the seat frame rails.

Now make the back stays, and check that 13¼in between the spigot shoulders on their dowel will allow everything to close easily inside the stays when the chair is assembled, (Figs. 8.1 and 8.5). When you are sure, or have adjusted the shoulder length as necessary, turn the ⁷/₁₆in spigots on the dowel. Make the curved metal stay (Fig. 8.7) but before you drill the rivet holes in it, check that it will control the closing of the chair so that the back stays come neatly outside and in line with the front legs. Glasspaper and wedge-glue the dowel between the back stays.

FINAL ASSEMBLY AND FINISHING

Now put the whole chair together, rivets, washers, and all, checking that it opens and closes well. All the rivets can next be cut off to length, but before doing so you must decide about the finish.

Assuming the chair will be used out of doors, you have the choice of oil, polyurethane (staining should not be necessary) or, of course, you can use one of the newer microporous varnish stains. My recipe for an oiled finish is to use boiled linseed oil plus 10% white spirit (mineral spirits) plus 5% (maximum) terebene – 15 to 20 coats rubbed on with a rag with 24 hours between each, which is tedious work but worth it in my opinion. If you use polyurethane it is advisable to apply it to the parts separately before finally riveting up. When the parts are ready to be put together, cut all the rivets to length and get someone to help you join it all up.

CUTTING LIST

	INCHES			MM		
	L	W	T	L	W	T
2 back upstands	18¼	1⅛	⅝	464	29	16
3 back rails	14	1¾	³/₁₆	355	45	5
1 back stay	15½	⅝ dia		394	16 dia	
2 front legs	15½	1⅛	⅝	394	29	16
2 sloping legs	19¼	1⅛	⅝	490	29	16
2 seat side rails	11½	2	⅝	292	51	16
2 seat dowels	13	⅝ dia		330	16 dia	
11 seat slats	11	1	³/₁₆	280	25	5
2 arms	13⅜	2¼	⅝	340	58	16
1 stiffener dowel	12	½ dia		305	12 dia	
1 front leg dowel	13½	⅝ dia		343	16 dia	
1 rear leg dowel	15½	⅝ dia		394	16 dia	

Metal parts not included.

Working allowances have been made to lengths and widths; thicknesses are net.

HEPPLEWHITE-STYLE CHAIR

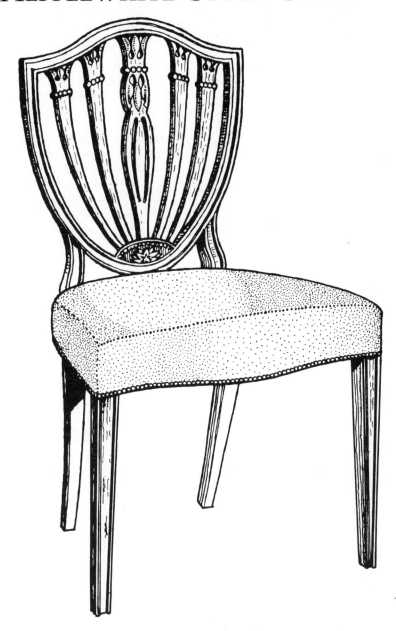

Hepplewhite would recognise this design as one of his! It's a simplified version of an armchair illustrated in Plate 9 of his *Cabinet Maker and Upholsterer's Guide*, published by his wife in 1788 after he died.

The decoratiye details are slightly different from the *Guide* illustration; the legs are square tapered instead of being turned, and the arms are omitted, but the overall similarity is there. Almost certainly it was made up by a chairmaker who altered the original design to suit his own skill and his customer's pocket. The function of such 'Guides' was to provide the craftsman with a basic idea that he could adapt to his own needs, and it's been said that the 'Guides' by such designers as Chippendale, Hepplewhite, Hope and so on – but possibly not Sheraton – provided so few details of construction, dimensions and shapes, that craftsmen of the time must have

been very highly skilled to have made them up at all.

This particular design is in mahogany and has a shaped banister with two vertical curved stays at each side of it, all meeting in a curved shoe at the foot of the shield back. The front face of the shield back frame is moulded (see the section in Fig. 9.2), while the back is benched (rounded off) all round. The front legs are square and tapered, with the outside faces moulded to the section given in Fig. 9.2. The seat is stuffover-upholstered, with a slightly serpentine shaped front rail.

You will need to take care with the joints, for the back in particular is quite delicate. You will also have to think carefully about the most economical way of marking and cutting the various curved members (Fig. 9.3B) to avoid short-grained pieces; the diagram shows the directions of the grain.

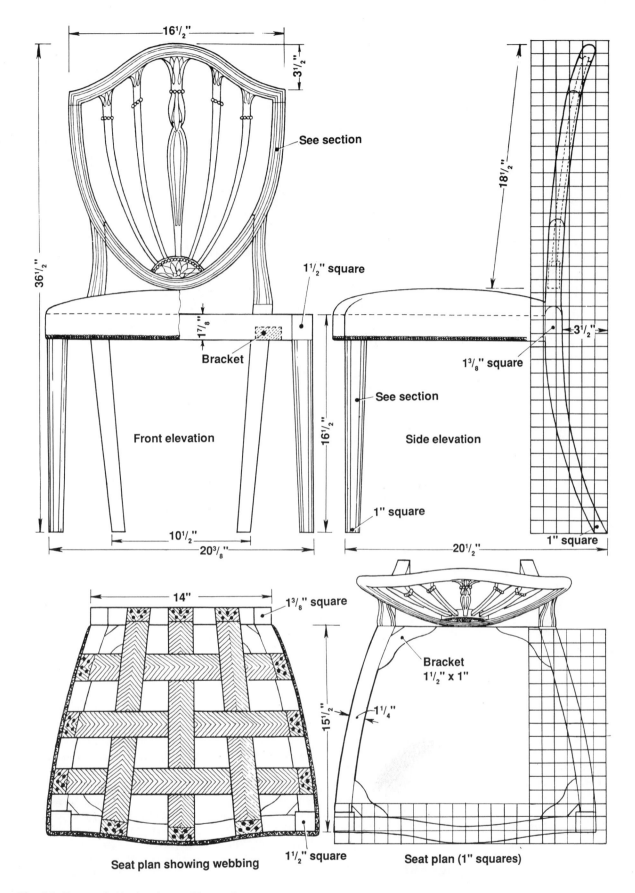

Fig. 9.1. Front and side elevations, with seat plans.

CONSTRUCTION

An exploded view of the chair with the parts in blank unworked form is shown in Fig. 9.3A, and you will see that the seat consists of a serpentine front rail, deep-cut from 2in wood to the shape shown in the plan (Fig. 9.1). The two slightly curved side seat rails are cut similarly while the back seat rail is straightforward. When marking out the various shapes, nest them together to save timber.

Mortise and tenon these rails into the front legs and backfeet; although plain stub-tenons are shown, you could mitre the ends of the tenons to meet inside the

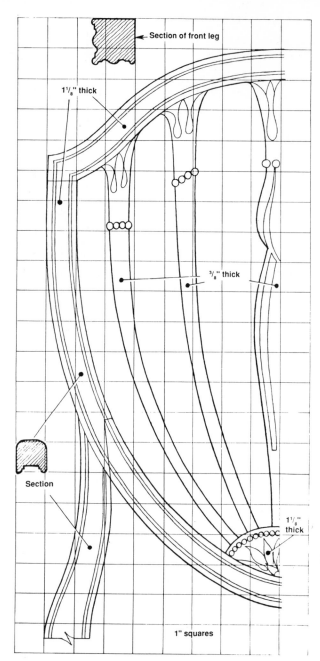

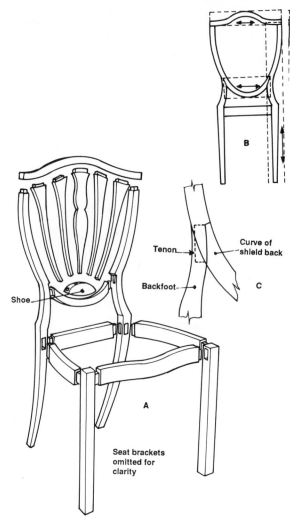

Fig. 9.3. Construction details.

Fig. 9.2. One-inch grid drawing of half of the back.

mortises. Save the offcuts when you cut the rails as they can be used as cramping blocks when you assemble the seat frame.

The backfeet are difficult to cut as they are curved in two planes. You will need two straight-grained pieces, each 3½in by 2½in by 36½in; bandsaw the shape as viewed from the front first, followed by the side profile (shown in the front and side elevations, Fig. 9.1). Again, keep the offcuts for use as cramping blocks.

The lower curved piece of the back is tenoned into a notch cut in each backfoot (Fig. 9.3C). This curved piece is grooved centrally to accept the tongue which is worked under the shoe, and this shoe is also mortised to accept the lower ends of the back stays; the stays are mortised in whole, without a tenon cut at the ends. The upper ends of the stays are tenoned into the underside of the top rail, which is serpentine-shaped (this type of top rail is often called a 'camel back'). Complete these joints before you start any carving; the size and shape of each stay is shown in Fig. 9.2.

Make tenons at the upper ends of the backfeet to fit into mortises on the underside of the top back rail. This rail is all in one plane, so it can be cut from 1¼in wood, saving the offcut again to act as a cramping block.

Details of the carving are shown in Fig. 9.2. Cut the channelling on the front legs with a router if you have one, or with a moulding plane; notice that the legs are slightly tapered. With the curves of the back frame you will probably have to resort to a scratch stock and a few carving tools such as a fine chisel and a suitable gouge. It is difficult to show the carving of the stylised husks, and it is a good idea to look at some actual examples in a museum, if you can.

Before you start the upholstery, glue and screw in the corner brackets (Fig. 9.1), locating them at the lower edges of the seat rails so they are clear of the webbing, and apply whatever finish you have chosen to the show wood parts.

UPHOLSTERY

Begin by webbing up the seat with the best quality

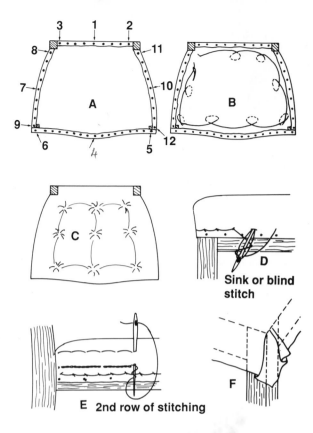

Fig. 9.4. Details of seat upholstery.

2in webbing, folding back the ends of the webs by about 1in to 1¼in and tacking through the double thickness. Use a webbing stretcher to apply tension, tacking down the central web first at the back and then at the front, and then continue with the rest, interlacing them as shown in Fig. 9.1, and using ½in tacks.

Now you have to cover the webs with hessian (Fig. 9.4A). Start by cutting out the piece of hessian about 1½in larger all round than the seat frame. Tack down the back edge, setting ½in tacks in about ⅜in from the edge of the hessian and following the sequence shown; pull the hessian as taut as possible before tacking. At the back corners, cut into the free part of the hessian at 45 degrees right up to the leg, then stretch the lips of the cut on either side of the leg and tack them down. Finally, trim the hessian to leave a surplus margin of about 1in wide all round, turning this margin inwards and tacking it down.

Upholstery fibre, readily available from upholstery suppliers, is one of the best stuffings for the seat. You will need to anchor it in place with 'bridle ties' (see Fig. 9.4B) positioned about 3in from the edge of the seat frame; these prevent the fibre from moving about in use and forming uncomfortable lumps or ridges.

Use an upholsterer's curved needle threaded with strong twine. Start by either of the back corners, making a small knot in the twine to stop it pulling through. The ties should be long enough so that there are two at each side and three along the front; the underside stitches (dotted in the diagram) need only be 1in or so long. Push handfuls of fibre under the ties, teasing it out until it covers the top to an even depth of about 4in and overhangs slightly all round. If necessary, fill in the centre with a small quantity of fibre.

Now cover all this stuffing with a piece of scrim

(hessian will do as an acceptable substitute) and fix it temporarily with part-driven tacks. Then stitch it down, using a straight mattress needle and twine, beginning about 4in inwards from the back leg, and pushing the needle down right through the scrim, the fibre, and the bottom hessian. Allow about an inch of stitching on the underside before pushing the needle up again and making a slip knot to tie the stitch. Continue around the seat, with long stitches on the top and small ones underneath, removing the temporary tacks as you go. Do not make any more slip knots until you come to the last stitch, which can be finished off with a slip knot close to the one you started with. Finally, trim off the edge of the scrim and tack it to the sides of the seat rails (Fig. 9.4C).

For the seat edge use a 'sink' or 'blind' stitch as shown in Fig 9.4D, employing a straight needle and twine. Start with a slip knot at the left-hand side close to the back foot and seat rail; push the needle through until the eye almost disappears, and then return it, pulling the knot tight. Take the needle along about 2½in, insert it again in a similar fashion, but return it about 1¼in behind the entry point. Twist the twine once around the needle as it emerges and pull it tight. Use a regulator (a stout knitting needle makes a good substitute) to adjust the amount of filling and keep it neat and even as you go.

Continue this process right round the seat. Then start another row of stitching about ½in above the first. For this row, thread the needle with twine and make the first stitch in one side of the seat about 1in from the backfoot and about 1½in from the edge. Bring the needle out about 1½in in from the edge on the top of the seat, and pull it right through. Then insert it again, eye first, close to the backfoot on the top of the seat, and pull it out at the side close to the loose end of the twine; make a slip knot to anchor the end. Next, insert the point of the needle about 1in along from the first stitch and again bring it out on top of the seat; wind the twine twice around the needle, bring it through and pull the stitch tight (Fig. 9.4E). Continue the stitching in this fashion all round the seat.

Upholstery fibre can also be used for the top stuffing, with bridle ties to hold it in place. Tease the fibre out evenly so it covers the seat about 1in deep, although it is helpful to have it slightly thicker at the front where the wear is greatest.

The seat should initially be covered with a piece of calico or other closely woven fabric to prevent any strands of fibre working through. Cut a piece large enough to cover the seat and hang down over the frame. Tack it to the outside of the back rail first, beginning at the centre and working outwards. Pull the calico taut and tack it to the front and side rails in a similar fashion. Align the tacks about ⅝in above the bottom edge of the seat rails and about ¾in apart. Fit the calico around the backfeet as you did with the hessian, and cut and fit it around the front legs (Fig. 9.4F) in the recognised method for negotiating this kind of corner. Finally, trim off the calico close to the tacks.

Before fitting the final cover, you should position a layer of cotton wadding about 1in thick on top of the calico, trimming it neatly at the corners. This wadding is held in place by the final cover, which you can now tack down in the same way as the calico. This cover must be large enough to cover not only the calico but also to lap over the undersides of the seat frame rails. When you have tacked it in place, on the undersides, insert some more tacks at about 1½in intervals around the bottom edges of the rails, below those holding the calico.

Complete the job by tacking on gimp with gimp pins to hide the tack heads. Then sit down and enjoy your chair!

CUTTING LIST

	INCHES			MM		
	L	W	T	L	W	T
2 backfeet from						
1 piece	34	6½	1⅜	864	165	35
2 front legs	17	1¾	1½	432	45	38
1 front seat rail	19	2¼	1	482	57	25

CUTTING LIST (continued)

	INCHES			MM		
	L	W	T	L	W	T
2 side seats rails from						
1 piece	16½	5½	1⅞	419	140	48
1 back seat rail	14	1½	1⅞	356	38	48
1 top crest rail	17	5⅛	1⅜	432	130	35
1 back bottom curve	14½	7	1⅛	368	178	29
1 centre splat	16	2¼	⅜	407	57	10
2 inner splats, each	16½	2¼	⅜	419	57	10
2 outer splats, each	15¾	2¾	⅜	400	70	10
1 shoe	4½	2	1⅛	115	51	29

Also required: 4 seat brackets from offcuts.
Working allowances have been made to lengths and widths; thicknesses are net.

GIMSON–STYLE LADDERBACK CHAIR

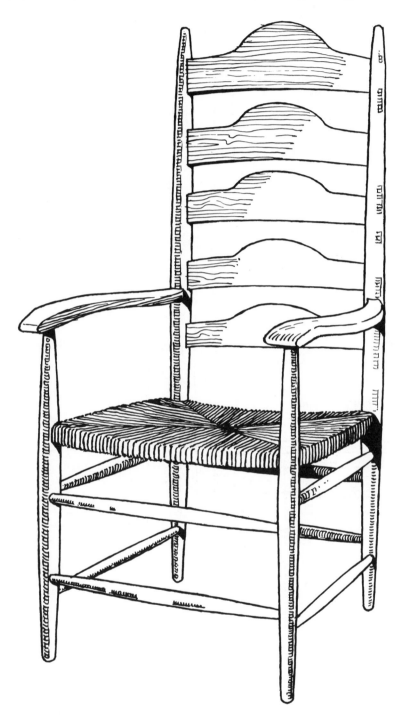

The original of this handsome chair is now in the Cheltenham Museum, England, in the section devoted to furniture made by Ernest Gimson and the brothers, Ernest and Sidney Barnsley. In fact, it was made in their Pinbury (Gloucestershire) workshop by Gimson about 1895 and then used by Sidney Barnsley in his own workshop.

GENERAL CONSTRUCTION
The chair is made in ash throughout and, although the construction should be obvious from the drawings, there are several points to note.

The front legs and underframe spars are straightforward turnery, but the backfeet will almost certainly be too long to turn between centres. This means shaping them by hand, which involves planing them as far as possible to a hexagonal section and then finishing them off with a drawknife or spokeshave.

Each backfoot will then need mortising to take the tenons on the ends of the ladder rails, and the mortises should be about ½in deep as shown in the front elevation Fig. 10.1. The end elevation of the same drawing shows that each ladder is set at a slight

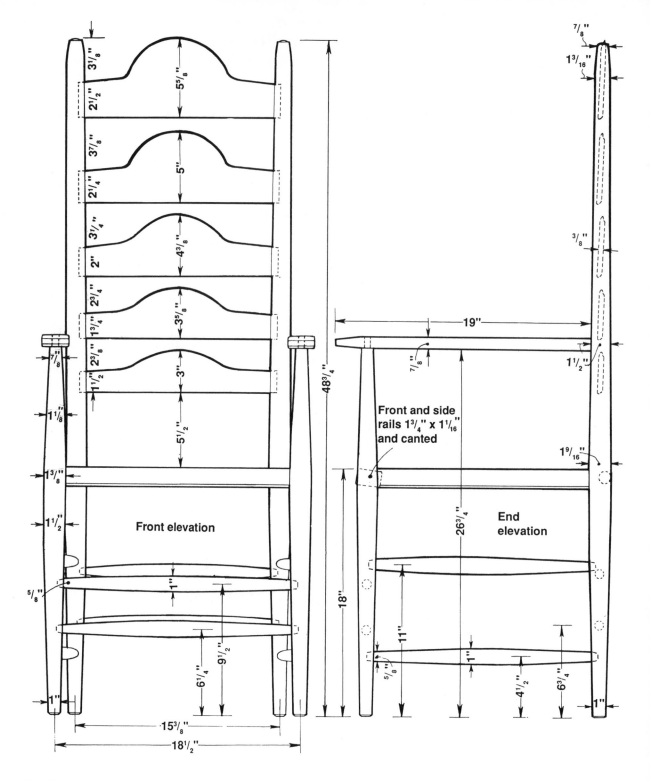

Fig. 10.1. Front and side elevations.

angle to the vertical, the angle being the same for each ladder.

As is usual with this type of chair, the underframe spars are mortised into the legs (Fig. 10.1, front elevation) and the front legs have pins turned on their upper ends which penetrate the arms and show on the upper surface.

ARMS AND LADDER RAILS
Fig. 10.2 shows the plan and section of an arm, which needs to be hand-benched to shape. It has a square ⅞in tenon on the back end which is mortised into the backfoot and pegged, with the head of the peg being allowed to show.

Also in Fig. 10.2 is an elevation of the top ladder rail, together with its section. Note that the bottom edge is rounded off while the top edge is profiled as shown. They are also slightly curved, and you may have to steam-bend them to shape, which should not be too difficult as ash bends readily.

SEAT
The trickiest part of the chair is the seat construction. The back seat rail is actually a turned cylinder, ¾in diameter, which is tenoned into the backfeet at each end – each tenon needs only to be a pin of, say, ½in diameter and ½in long. The side and front rails are bareface-tenoned into the backfeet and the front legs;

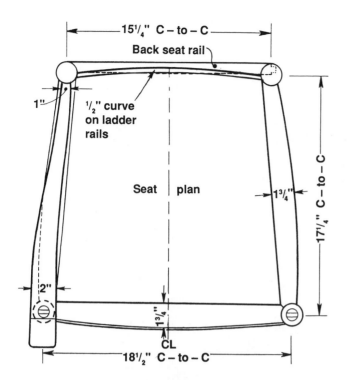

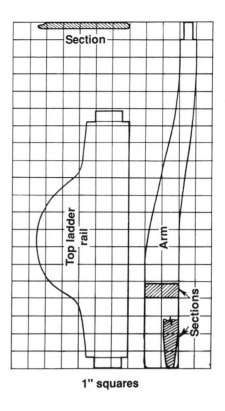

Fig. 10.2. Seat plan and one-inch grid drawing of shapes for ladder rail and arm.

the most important feature is that they are all canted at a slight angle from the horizontal as shown in the end elevation, Fig 10.1. Note, too, that their outside edges are slightly curved as shown in the seat plan, Fig. 10.2.

Not having learnt to rush-seat chairs, I am not qualified to give any instructions about it. Unless you are experienced in such work, you would be well-advised to put it out to a local craftsman; also quite often there are institutions for the blind that specialise in this kind of work.

FINISH

A chair like this, which has a definite 'country' air about it, is probably best finished with a simple wax polish. To do this, start by giving it a good coat of shellac (clear French polish) which will seal the end grain and help to prevent grime from entering the grain, and then apply any good proprietary wax polish, which must be non-silicone. Thereafter it's a matter of frequent applications plus plenty of elbow grease.

CUTTING LIST

	INCHES			MM		
	L	W	T	L	W	T
2 backfeet	49¼	1¾ dia		1250	45 dia	
2 front legs	28⅛	1⅝ dia		714	41 dia	
2 arms	19⅞	2¼	⅞	505	58	22
1 ladder rail No 1	15¾	5⅞	⅜	400	150	10
1 ladder rail No 2	15⅝	5¼	⅜	397	133	10
1 ladder rail No 3	15½	4⅝	⅜	394	118	10
1 ladder rail No 4	15⅜	3⅞	⅜	391	99	10
1 ladder rail No 5	15⅜	3¼	⅜	391	83	10
1 front underframe spar	18½	1¼ dia		470	32 dia	
1 front underframe spar	18¾	1¼ dia		476	32 dia	
1 back underframe spar	15¾	1¼ dia		400	32 dia	
1 back underframe spar	15½	1¼ dia		394	32 dia	
2 side spars	17½	1¼ dia		445	32 dia	
2 side spars	17⅜	1¼ dia		442	32 dia	
1 back seat rail	15¼	1 dia		387	25 dia	
2 side seat rails	17½	2	1¹⁄₁₆	445	51	27
1 front seat rail	18¼	2	1¹⁄₁₆	464	51	27

Working allowances have been made to lengths and widths; thicknesses are net.

Chippendale Library Chair

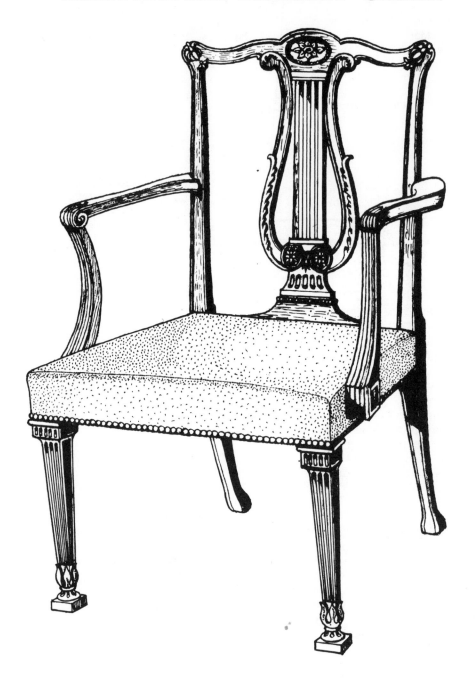

This distinguished lyre-back library chair is from a set of six which have a documented provenance, having been made by Thomas Chippendale, senior, for the library at Lord Melbourne's country house about 1773. The set was sold to an American at the Brocket Hall sale in 1923. They disappeared from view until one surfaced in New York in 1976 and was acquired by the Chippendale Society with the aid of grants from the government, the National Art-Collections Fund and the Pilgrim Trust. It is now on loan to Temple Newsam House, Leeds, England, and its companions are reputed to be in various private collections on Long Island, USA.

The lyre-back design was first used by Chippendale for a set of six chairs he supplied in 1768 for the library at Nostell Priory, near Wakefield, Yorkshire (at a cost of £6 each), where they still remain. The set commissioned by Lord Melbourne, although less richly carved, is more fluent, and in fact is one of Chippendale's most eloquent designs. He traded at the Sign of the Chair in St Martin's Lane, London, which suggests that the firm enjoyed a high reputation for its seat furniture.

Details of the chair are reproduced by courtesy of the Chippendale Society.

SHAPING THE BACK

The flowing lines of the piece may well cause the would-be chairmaker to groan in anticipation of hours of work spent in benching the compound

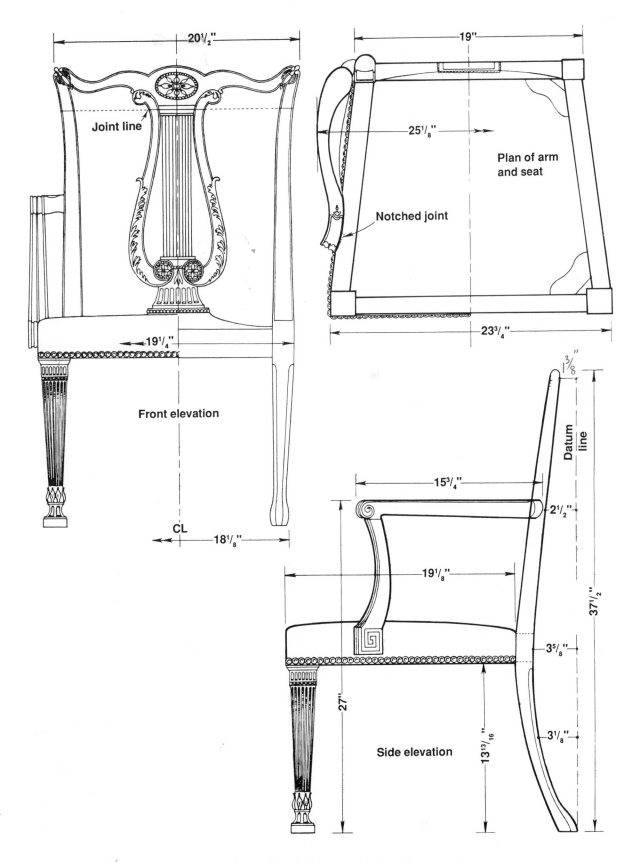

Fig. 11.1. Front elevation and plan of seat and arm; also side elevation with datum line.

curves which normally accompany this kind of design. Surprisingly, there are none – the top rail (which is here called the crest rail), the lyre motif banister, the arms, and the stumps are all flat and in one plane.

Such shaping as there is on the face of the crest rail can be achieved by shaping and rounding-off its upper edge down to a thickness of about ⁵⁄₁₆in from the full finished thickness of ⁵⁄₈in.

From the original, it appears that the two carved bosses at the bottom curves of the lyre motif in the banister were carved out of the solid. As each boss stands proud of the surrounding surface by about ³⁄₁₆in, it would involve quite a waste of timber to clear away the wood locally, particularly when you realise that each boss could be turned up as a separate item and glued on prior to carving, just as you would deal with a patera.

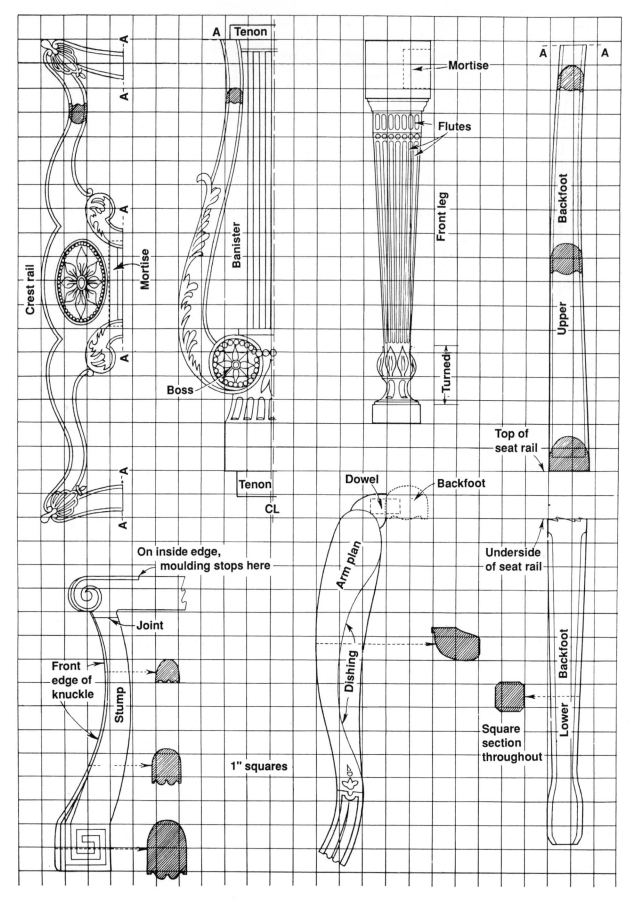

Fig. 11.2. Details of shaped and decorated parts on one-inch grid.

SHAPING THE ARM AND STUMP

The shape of the arm is as you would expect for the period and style. On the outer edge the wood is taken away to leave a ³⁄₁₆in moulding along the top edge; this moulding tapers away at the junction with the backfoot and terminates with a scroll at the front. There is a similar scroll at the front on the inside of the arm, but here the moulding stops at the point shown in Fig. 11.2, and then the dishing of the arm starts.

The 'knuckle' moulding on the front face of the stump stands forward about ¼in and this has to be allowed for when considering the size of the timber from which the stump is to be cut. Note also the Grecian key motif at the bottom of the stump; this feathers out at the front edge.

LEGS AND BACKFEET
The front legs are straightforward enough; they are square in section with the exception of the bulbs just above the block feet at the bottom.

The backfeet are a different proposition as they are angled in two planes. A side elevation is shown in Fig. 11.1 and you will see that a vertical datum line is given with the dimensioned variations from it; this should enable you to plot the shape. Fig. 11.2 shows the front elevation. Although the upper half of the backfoot is heavily rounded off on the back, the lower half is square in section with the arrises bevelled off.

A point to note in Fig. 11.1 is that the two backfeet toe-in quite considerably – this is a feature in many good chair designs. Often it can be troublesome, as it means that the shoulders of the seat rail joints have to be angled slightly to give the toe-in. But in this design it is unnecessary as the inward splay is brought about by tapering the outer face while the inner face is kept vertical.

JOINTS AND CONSTRUCTION
We come now to the general consideration of the construction and joints, as shown in Fig. 11.3. The front and side seat rails can be mortised and tenoned into the legs (see H and I) and, of course, the seat brackets help to strengthen the joints.

Obviously, it was impossible to dismember the actual chair to examine the construction, and the following methods are accepted chairmaking prac-

tice. This means that although the seat side rails can be tenoned into the backfeet, it is advisable to dowel the seat back rail in place (see K), arranging the dowels so that they pierce the tenons on the side rails and pin them. This will make for a strong joint at the most vulnerable point of the chair, and the seat brackets will provide further reinforcement.

The banister (sometimes called a 'splat') can be slotted into a mortise in the seat back rail (F) and strengthened by a shoe (E) which is notched on its back edge to fit around the banister. This shoe is itself pinned and glued down on the upper edge of the seat rail.

When jointing on the stump you will find that it will have to be cut away at the bottom to fit over the seat rail, which needs to be recessed to accept it (G). The stump meets the rail at a slight angle which will have to be allowed for when recessing.

At its front end, the arm can be fixed with a loose dowel into the top of the stump (D), and can be similarly dowelled into the side of the backfoot (C) at its other end. The jointing of the crest rail on to the upper ends of the backfeet and on to the banister can be seen at (A) and (B).

Cramping up the joints is likely to be tricky because of the curved shapes of the various parts. The secret is to keep the offcuts handy, as you will find them invaluable as cramping-up blocks when you are dealing with the arms, stumps, banister, and crest rail.

UPHOLSTERY
The actual chair has stuff-over upholstery in leather with brass close-nailing around the front and the two sides. Probably the original upholstery was also stuff-over with a fabric cover over a down or hair filling; no doubt the filling would have been stitched to webbing and also buttoned to prevent it from moving.

FINISHING
The chair is made in mahogany (most likely Honduras) which allows close-fitting joints, plus strength combined with comparatively slender sections. If you are going to make the chair you will need to choose a good quality hardwood such as abura, agba or guarea.

These are all of a colour which can be stained to resemble true mahogany and they are not so likely to have the interlocked grain of woods like sapele, which would make carving really difficult.

The following are Thomas Sheraton's instructions for polishing: "Chairs are generally polished with a hardish composition of wax rubbed on with a polishing brush [probably the kind used for cleaning footwear today] with which the grain of wood is impregnated with the composition, and afterwards well rubbed off . . . The composition I recommend is as follows: take beeswax and a small quantity of turpentine in a clean earthen pan and set it over a fire [from the point of view of fire risk, we would recommend putting it into a heat-resistant glass basin and standing it in a pan of boiling water] till the wax unites with the turpentine, which it will do by constantly stirring about; add to this a little red lead finely ground upon a stone, together with a small portion of fine Oxford ochre to bring the whole to the colour of brisk mahogany [today we would use powder colours]. Lastly, when you take it off the

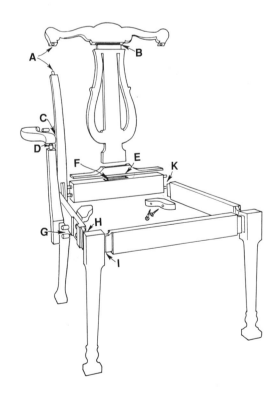

Fig. 11.3. Construction and joints.

fire, add a little copal varnish to it, and mix it well together, then turn the whole into a basin of water, and while it is yet warm, work it into a ball, with which the brush is to be rubbed as before observed."

Although Sheraton lived at a slightly later date than Chippendale, there is no reason to think that the method of polishing had changed.

CUTTING LIST

	INCHES			MM		
	L	W	T	L	W	T
2 front legs	16½	3⅛	2⅞	419	80	73
2 backfeet	38	6	1⅞	965	153	48
1 front seat rail	24	2⅝	1½	609	67	38

CUTTING LIST (continued)

	INCHES			MM		
	L	W	T	L	W	T
2 side seat rails	21	2⅝	1½	533	67	38
1 back seat rail	16	2⅝	1½	406	67	38
2 arms	16½	3	1¾	419	76	45
2 stumps	11⅛	3½	1⅞	283	89	48
1 banister or splat	20½	9	⅝	521	229	16
1 top crest rail	21	4	1	553	102	25
1 shoe	16	2	1½	406	51	38

Also required: seat brackets from offcuts.
Working allowances have been made to lengths and widths; thicknesses are net.

PEG-LEGS AND SGABELLE

(A) Italian sgabelle, 15th century; (B) German-American chair about 1850; (C) Swiss plank-back; (D) German 18th century chair with pierced strapwork.

When is a chair not a chair? And when is a stool not a stool? When it's a peg-leg, sgabelle, spindle, stick, spinning, Orkney or a slab-back seat.

If you are still no wiser, picture the simple, traditional milkmaid's stool – three or four legged, it makes no matter. Add an upright plank back, a handful of wedges and a bit of shallow relief carving. Before you can say 'rustic' and 'belonging to the peasant tradition', you have the basic, archetypal cottage chair.

Chairs of this type and character cannot be described as belonging to specific countries or periods.

Fig. 12.1. Inspiration from some seats and backs in the European folk tradition.

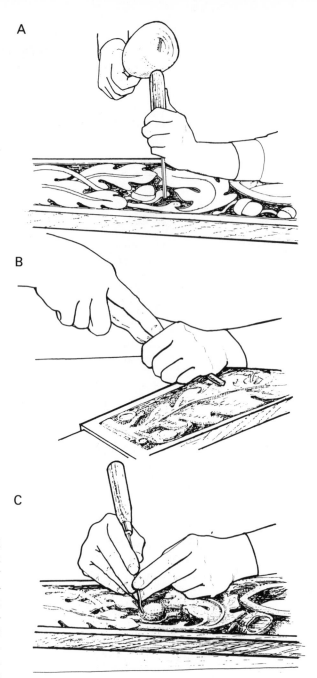

Fig. 12.2. (A) After drawing out the design, cut a V-section trench round it and set in with a straight chisel and gouge. Round the edges of the relief forms, (B) and then dish them by scooping from side to centre to create a rippled effect. Finally, (C) add the details, tidy up the carving and generally pull it all together.

All we can say for sure is that they are found wherever there is a peasant, folk-primitive, 'kitchen hearth', furniture-making tradition. In colonial New England there were beautiful plank-seated, stick-legged, wedge-tenoned chairs known as 'peg-legs'; in Renaissance Italy they were somewhat over-carved, three-legged, scroll-backed seats known as 'sgabelles'. Closer to home in Scotland and northern Europe, there were plank-backed chairs known variously as 'Orkney', 'spinning', and 'spindle' stools – and so I could go on, with examples from Russia, Scandinavia, Switzerland and Germany.

Peg-legs and plank-backs are essentially humble, rustic and home-made, and therein lies their naive and honest charm. What's more, of course, you don't need a fancy tool kit, and there aren't any 'high tec' joints, screws, nails, glue or suchlike; just slab wood and simple, direct easy-to-manage techniques. You won't finish up with a gesso encrusted baroque cabriole legged carver (or even, for that matter, a particularly comfortable chair); but you will be able to let rip with your own idiosyncratic design ideas, and get to grips with some honest-to-goodness making and carving.

I reckon that this project can be undertaken by the keen beginner in a couple of weekends.

TOOLS AND MATERIALS

Before you start, throw away most of your preconceived ideas of how a chair ought to be made, and try to feel yourself into the shoes of a never-done-it-before pioneer or peasant woodworker. You're using in-the-rough or found wood, you only have a few basic tools, and you are seeking, to the best of your ability, to make a simple, strong, serviceable and decorative chair.

Get yourself a slab of rough-sawn 1½in half-seasoned oak, and make sure that it's reasonably straightgrained and free from warps, splits, shakes, and dead knots. A board 42in long, 12in wide and 1 to 2 in thick will do just fine. This chair, as illustrated in the gridded working drawings, has a seat 12in by 13in; the plank back is 27in long including the tenon, and tapers from 6 to 8in wide at the top to about 4in wide at the tenon shoulders; and there are four tapered octagonal-sectioned legs. As for tools, you need a large coping or bow saw, a mallet, a brace or hand drill, a spokeshave or draw knife, a straight chisel, a straight gouge, a V-section tool, a spoon bit chisel, a spoon bit gouge, and of course such 'around the workshop' items as pencils, a measure, set of compasses, a square, a cramp, and rough working-out paper.

FIRST STEPS AND MARKING OUT

Have a good look at our working drawings and inspirational ideas, give your wood a last check, and with the compasses, measure and pencil, start to set out the design, as illustrated.

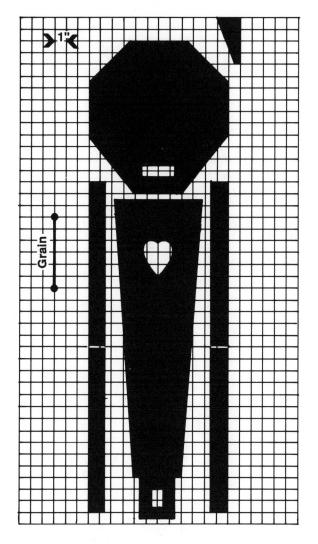

Fig. 12.3. One-inch grid diagram providing a well proportioned layout for all the component parts of the chair.

Measure and mark the eight-side seat slab, the four legs, the plank back, and the seat. When you're sure that all is correct, clearly label the blanks. If you like the overall design but would prefer a taller back, a wider seat, or whatever, now's the time to adjust the chair to suit your needs. Finally, cut out the blanks with a fine-toothed straight saw.

SETTING OUT AND CARVING

Before you start setting out the area to be carved, take each piece, secure it to the bench with the cramp, and with a shallow gouge bring its surface to a slightly rippled finish. Don't aim for a characterless 'plastic' smoothness – rather a soft, dappled and gently scalloped tooled texture.

Next, with the compasses and straightedge, set out the areas for carving. Have a good look at the

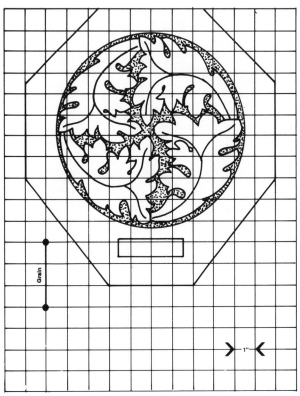

Fig. 12.4. This is a one-inch grid drawing of the seat design we evolved for this particular project.

gridded drawings and see how the design of the 9in diameter seat roundel is quartered, and set back about 1¼in from the front edge of the seat slab. Notice also how the plank-back design is organised, pierced, and contained within a border.

THE PLANK-BACK

Once you have drawn out the design you can start to work the back. With the wood secure in the vice, take the coping-saw and hand drill and work the pierced heart motif. Drill a starter hole and then, with the coping saw blade at 90 degrees to the working surface, cut out the heart. Work with an even and steady stroke, manoeuvring and turning the saw as you go.

Then clamp the wood flat and square on the work bench and arrange your chisels and gouges so that they are comfortably to hand. Re-check the design, and with a pencil re-establish its lines and black in the areas that need to be lowered.

Now take the V-section tool and start to outline the whole of the design – all the time working on the waste or ground side, and cutting into the wood about ¼in outside the drawn lines. As you work the V-section incised trench you will be cutting both with and across the grain, so hold the tool with both hands, one guiding and one pushing; work with short, shallow, controlled strokes, and be ready to stop short if you feel the tool running into the grain or skidding out of control. At this stage you shouldn't need to use a mallet; just put your shoulder behind the tool and try to cut a smooth V-section trench, not too deep.

When you've outlined the design, go round the drawn lines and 'set in' with the straight chisel and gouge. Hold the tool in one hand so that the handle is leaning slightly over the design, and cut into the lines of the motif with short lively taps of the mallet.

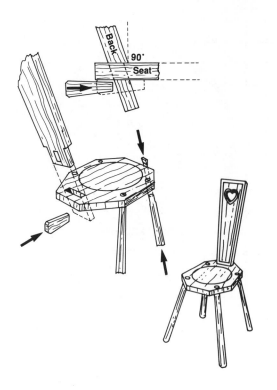

Look at the acorns-and-oak-leaves design, as illustrated, and see how the forms have been worked in a rather formal and mechanical manner. Take the straight gouge and work round the raised design, all the while cutting away and rounding the sharp edges. Don't even attempt to carve subtle realism and complex undercuts; rather go for swift and direct stylisation. When you have rounded the edges of the motifs, dish them gently – scoop out the wood from side to centre, all the time taking care that you don't damage shortgrain areas or cut into the raised leaf veining.

And so you continue to work; cutting and running the tools across the grain, and over and around the forms, until you feel that you have taken the carving as far as you want it to go. Don't fuss and worry the design; try to keep it simple and bold. When you have worked the plank-back, work the seat roundel in like manner.

Fig. 12.5. The plank-back tenon is clamped firmly by a wedge; the mortise in the seat is angled. Four more wedges secure the legs.

THE MORTISES AND TENONS
If you look closely at the plank-back-to-seat joint, you will see that the tapered plank is tenoned and rebated so that it enters the seat mortise at an oblique angle of about 100–110 degrees. Once the plank-back tenon and seat mortise have been cut and worked to fit, the rebated shoulders of the tenon need to be pared and bevelled until they strike the seat smooth and clean.

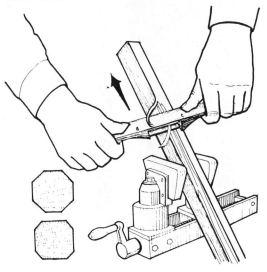

Fig. 12.6. (A) Setting up the coping saw for piercing the back. (B) a spokeshave, draw knife, or a plane tapers the legs and takes them down to an octagonal section – regular or otherwise.

Try all the time to keep the depth of cut constant, say ⅛ to ¼in, and aim to establish a clean, sharp-edged design. The setting-in should follow the V-trench and the edge of the design in a single, smooth and continuous line.

Some carvers lower or 'waste' the unwanted 'ground' of the design before they set in. Alternatively, you can do this now. Take the spoon-bit gouge, cut a broad trench on the ground side of the V-section cut, and – when you have established the depth of the lowered ground – chop out the whole area. Try to leave the lowered ground smooth and even, but not so overworked that you can't see the tool marks. Finally, work round the now-raised motifs and make sure the angles are free from bits and burrs.

This done, cut a slot in the plank-back tenon, at an angle parallel to the seat, and then cut and fit a wedge as illustrated.

CUTTING AND FIXING THE LEGS
Take the 14in long leg blanks, a stick at a time, secure them in the vice and then shape them with a spokeshave or draw knife until they are gently tapered and octagonal in section. Aim to take the taper from about 1½in at the bottom to about 1¼in at the top.

When you've done four legs, place the carved seat slab face down on the work bench and bore four angled holes. Then continue to work the tapered ends of the legs until they are a good stiff fit in the bored seat holes.

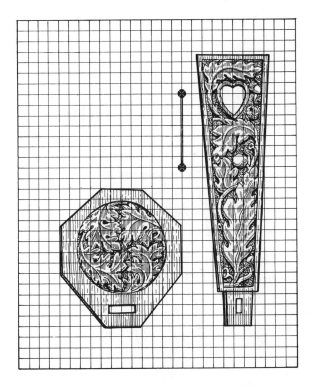

Fig. 12.7. One-inch grid drawing of the seat roundel and the plank back. We chose an oak tree theme but you are, of course, free to choose a design of your own.

Finally, when the legs fit flush with the seat, make the joints as shown.

GETTING IT ALL TOGETHER

When the legs have been wedge-tenoned into the seat and the plank-back tenon inserted into the mortise, its holding wedge can be banged home. Adjust the chair so that it sits firm and foursquare, and go over your work with a small gouge tidying up sharp edges and making sure all the surfaces have a dappled, tooled texture.

Finally, remove all the dust and wood fragments with a stiff brush, give it a couple of coats of beeswax, and the job is done.

On traditional peg-leg chairs of this character the carving is usually incised or shallow relief, but of course there's no reason why the chair shouldn't be painted, chip-carved or whatever takes your fancy.

SOME OTHER POINTS

When you come to fixing the leg wedge-tenons, make sure the little wedges are cut in so that they run across the grain of the seat, as illustrated.

If you think the 1½in thick slab seat looks a little on the heavy side, bevel the edge of the underside with a gouge so that, edge-on, the seat looks to be about ¾in thick.

When you bore the leg holes in the seat slab, watch out that you don't split or damage the wood. It's a good idea to drill from both sides.

COUNTRY STYLE, HEPPLEWHITE CHAIR

Going round an auction recently, I came across the original of this chair. It was listed as 'Hepplewhite Style' which to my way of thinking needed the prefix 'Country'. It required quite a bit of renovation, including the tightening up of one arm stump and a new drop-in seat frame. Nevertheless, it had at one time obviously been a sturdy and comfortable chair.

A quick sketch and an equally quick run round with a rule, noting the principal dimensions, gave me enough information to go to work on. Minor details had to be memorized, and the fact that I began the job at once while these were fresh in my mind helped, perhaps, to produce the satisfactory job illustrated. Certainly some of the old chair makers knew

how to design chairs with style, strength, and comfort, qualities not so evident in much modern work!

PLANNING

The first thing I did was to draw a full-size seat plan; on this I superimposed the back elevation. The side elevation was then drawn, again full size. When I got the arm and stump shapes to my liking the two drawings were then linked in with a fibre tipped pen (leaving the seat plan in pencil).

I was now able to stand up the drawings on the floor and view them at a reasonable distance; at this stage they looked quite good. The only parts not fully shown were the arms in plan and their top

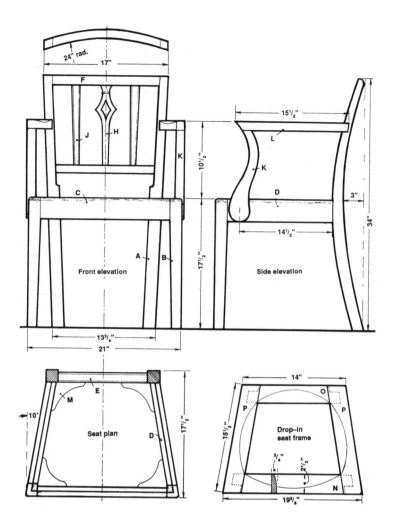

Fig. 13.1. Front and side elevations, with seat plan and details of drop-in seat.

shaping and these I decided to leave until the main framework was completed. Fig. 13.1 shows these drawings re-made and I would certainly recommend you to re-draw them out full size. All the angles will be shown and they can be transferred to a sliding bevel gauge for setting out as and when required.

Chair making of this kind is rather different from straight cabinet work – in the past it was considered a craft on its own. Compound angles are involved in most of the mortise and tenon joints and, while experienced workers will have no difficulty, for the less experienced the old adage of 'measure twice and cut once' could be re-written to read 'think thrice, measure twice, and cut once'!

TO WORK

I was now ready to start. Obviously, the first thing to do was to work the four legs (A) and (B). I was fortunate in having by me a length of 7in square mahogany sufficient to cut the backfeet, (A). I cut out a template for one backfoot from hardboard; this enabled me to confirm that the two could be cut side by side within the 7in width and still allow some manoeuvring to get the grain direction to favour the curves.

The next thing to do was to saw off a slice 1¾in thick – some job in a small workshop! My (nominally) 8in saw blade, after some years of sharpening, now only projects through the table 2¼in, so a cut from each side left 2½in in the middle to be ripsawn by hand. First, though, I surfaced three sides of the 'billet' on the planer; this exposed the grain and

enabled me, by means of the template, to choose the most suitable face to use. After sawing off, the piece was thickness to 1⅝in. Incidentally, the trued-up surfaces proved very useful later when I came to the final shaping and setting out the various mortises.

Using the template, I next marked out and sawed the two backfeet to shape on the bandsaw. A point to note here that may not at first be obvious is that it is necessary to allow for later shaping in plan to follow the curve of the top back rail (F). This means that the top end of each backfoot in side elevation should not be less than 1⅝in. This is shown in Fig. 13.2, and marked 'sectional plan on A-B'.

Next came the reduction of the upper part of the backfeet in front elevation to 1¼in (which starts 1½in above the top of the seat rail line) and this was sawn away and cleaned up.

For cleaning up the curves below the bottom rail (G), I used a Stanley compass plane. This is a plane with a flexible steel sole that can be bent (within limits) either convex or concave to suit the curve being worked, and is a very useful tool for jobs of this kind. Failing this, you can of course, use a spokeshave or a drawknife.

Now I had to plane a flat on each leg to provide a seating for the side seat rail shoulders. These flats must be identical on each leg or the side rails will not marry up in line at assembly time. They should be 3in long, extending below the top seat rail line, and to ensure accuracy I cramped both legs together while doing the job.

Following this, I marked out and cut the various

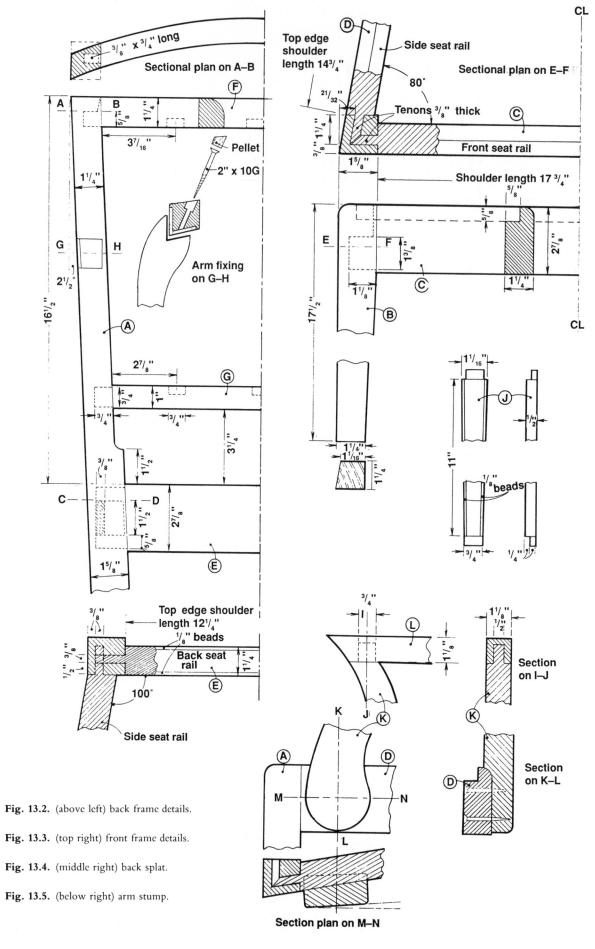

Fig. 13.2. (above left) back frame details.

Fig. 13.3. (top right) front frame details.

Fig. 13.4. (middle right) back splat.

Fig. 13.5. (below right) arm stump.

Within figure:

Sectional plan on A–B

$^3/_8$" x $^3/_4$" long

Top edge shoulder length 14$^3/_4$"

Side seat rail

Sectional plan on E–F

80°

Tenons $^3/_8$" thick

21/$_{32}$"

Front seat rail

Pellet

2" x 10G

Arm fixing on G–H

Shoulder length 17 $^3/_4$"

Arm fixing on G–H

Top edge shoulder length 12$^1/_4$"

$^1/_8$" beads

Back seat rail

100°

Side seat rail

$^1/_8$" beads

Section on I–J

Section on K–L

Section plan on M–N

mortises; reference to Fig. 13.2 gives their positions and sizes. Note that the side rail mortise is set vertically – not in line with the side of the backfoot – the angle being approximately 2½ degrees. Note, too, that all three back rail tenons enter the legs at this same angle off the true right angle; that is, 87½ degrees measured below the rails. I worked the mortises with a hollow chisel mortiser, and the correct angle was obtained by using a tapered packing piece below the leg. A taper of just over ½in to the foot will give the necessary 2½ degrees.

FRONT LEGS
Details of these are shown in Fig. 13.3. After I had sawn them out to 1¾in square, I surfaced them on two sides to 90 degrees and then thicknessed them to 1⅝in on the planer.

Before putting on the tapers, which was also done on the planer, I cut the mortises. The mortise for the side rail (D) is set in to allow for the later planing of the bevel (in plan) to follow the side seat rail angle, which is 10 degrees, but this is not done until after the rail has been trial-fitted. Bear in mind that this mortise is at 80 degrees to the front; two 10-degree tapered blocks when gripping the leg in the mortiser vice – take care of this. Details of this and the front rail joint are shown at Fig. 13.3, marked 'sectional plan on E-F'.

SEAT RAILS
Details of the four seat rails, (C), (D), and (E), are shown in Figs. 13.2 and 13.3. After sawing out, I planed and thicknessed them to 1¼in by 2⅞in. All tenons have ¼in haunches.

The tenons on the side rails (D), which enter the backfeet are not in line and are, in fact, canted outwards by 10 degrees. Another point to note is that the shoulders here are at 100 degrees (in plan) to the face and similarly the front shoulders on these are at 80 degrees, the tenon in this case being in line.

The shoulders of the back rail (E) are, of course, at 90 degrees in plan but in elevation they are at 87½ degrees, and two ⅛in beads are worked on the top edge of this rail. The joints of the front rail (C), are straightforward, having normal 90 degree shoulders.

Trial fitting of the rails (D) to the backfeet will show the amount of waste to be removed from the faces to blend in with the slope of the leg, but when you are planing to do this, it should not extend forward along the rail face beyond the back of the arm stump.

My next step was to work the rebate for the drop-in seat frame in rails (C) and (D), followed by working the quarter-round moulding on the outer top edges. At this stage I found it worthwhile to clear the bulk of the waste from the tops of the front legs so that I could continue the seat rail rebates into the corners, but I left a little waste for final finishing after gluing up. The stage was now reached where the front frame could be glued and cramped up.

BACK RAILS
Details of these, (F) and (G), are shown in Fig. 13.2 and 13.6. First, I dry-assembled the two backfeet with the seat rail E, and cramped them up; this enabled me to measure the exact shoulder lengths of (F) and (G). A small discrepancy may appear here compared with those shown on the drawing – this is not important provided that it is no more than ¼in or so on the top rail; otherwise the shoulder angle (in elevation) of the seat rail (E), should be adjusted slightly.

I continued by cutting out the rails on the bandsaw and cleaning the curves to their final sizes with a compass plane. Cutting the tenons came next, followed by the mortises for the back splats. Normally I cut my tenons on the planer, but this could not be done here for obvious reasons, so they had to be done by hand. First I used a craft knife to cut the shoulders in deeply all round, and then I pared a bevelled step on the waste side to the knife cut. This is a good idea as it provides a convenient shoulder against which to start the saw, much preferable to starting the saw directly in the knife cut, and it also creates a cleaner shoulder.

I then made a trial assembly of the back frame which enabled me to measure the exact shoulder length of the back splats. Again, there may be a slight discrepancy with those shown in the drawing, where I made an extra-generous allowance.

Details of the side splats are shown in Fig. 13.4, (J), and of the centre one in Fig. 13.6. During the trial assembly, I took the opportunity to mark the waste to be cut from the upper part of the backfeet. The bulk of this waste can be most conveniently removed before gluing up the frame, take care, though, to leave a small amount for final shaping after the gluing up which was done next, using tapered blocks on which to apply the cramps. After the glue had set, final cleaning up was done.

ASSEMBLY
I then made a trial assembly of the back and front frames with the side rails, to check that all joints would come together closely and that the seat frame was not in winding. At this stage, too, I marked the bevel necessary on the outer side of the front legs to bring them into line with the side rails. I then dismantled the frame and planed these bevels, again leaving a small allowance for finishing after gluing up. You will find it useful to cramp a 3in by 2in batten across the back frame at seat rail height as this will enable you to apply the back-to-front cramps squarely.

Once the glue had set, the four corner braces (M) were glued and screwed into position with their tops level with the seat frame rebate. Following this, I worked the top corners of the front legs to complete the quarter-round moulding along the seat rails; for this I used a small finely set block plane, finishing with glasspaper wrapped around a suitably shaped block.

ARMS AND ARM STUMPS
These are marked (K) and (L) and are shown in Figs. 13.5 and 13.6. To deal with the stumps (K) first; after I had sawn them out they were cleaned up to the outline. My disc and belt sanders made short work of this, and I used the drum end of the belt to work into the curves. Next, I cut the laps to fit to the side seat rails; this is shown in Fig. 13.5, at 'section K-L' and 'section plan M-N'. The lap is tapered in plan to bring the top of the arm stump in line with the arm.

The arms (L) were the next job. Fig. 13.5 gives details of the arm-to-stump joint, and details of the arm-to-back joint are shown in the inset drawing, Fig. 13.2 – the arm joint here is housed into the backfoot to a depth of ⅛in. A slight complication arises, in that the fixing screw has to enter more or less end grain so when I did the job I inserted a glued-in fibre plug into the screw hole.

After the joint had been satisfactorily dry-fitted to bring the front end of the arm in line with the top of the stump, I marked out and cut the necessary mortises and tenons. Another trial assembly confirmed that all parts would come together nicely, so

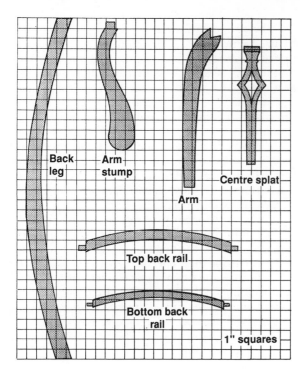

Fig. 13.6. One-inch grid drawing of shaped parts.

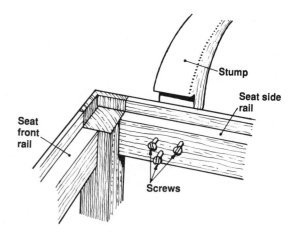

Fig. 13.7. Fixing the arm stump to the seat side rail.

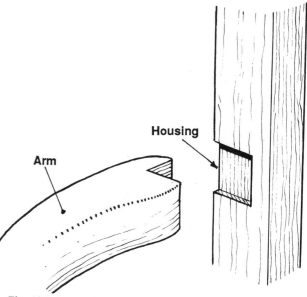

Fig. 13.8. Housing the arm to the backfoot.

the arm to stump joints were glued and put aside for the glue to set.

DROP-IN SEAT FRAME

You can see details of this in Fig. 13.1; I made mine in mild straightgrained oak, but any strong hardwood would be suitable.

Although the half-lap joint construction is often used, I prefer mortise and tenon jointing as there is less likelihood of the frame distorting under the strain of the webbing, and less chance of splitting at the corners when the upholstery tacks are driven in.

I allowed an ⅛in clearance all round the frame to accommodate the thickness of the upholstery and this proved to be just about right when a velveteen-style cover was used.

FINISHING

The first stage in this procedure is to look for any tiny bruises, scratches, planing tears and the like – these all have to be removed completely as they always show up worse once the finish has been applied.

Next, I gave the whole chair a thorough glasspapering, working through the sequence from medium to fine grades. I followed this by wiping the chair over with a cloth dampened with water; this raises the grain which then needs a further light papering to cut it back.

You have now reached the point where you have to decide whether to stain or not – a decision for you alone! If you do use a water stain, remember that it will once again raise the grain a little, which will have to be cut back as before.

I decided not to stain but to give the chair the traditional wipe over with boiled linseed oil, which does undoubtedly enrich the grain figure. After the oil had been given a few days in a dust-free atmosphere to dry out so that the chair could be handled, I applied a brush-coat of clear French polish (shellac). When this was dry, I rubbed it down well with finest grade steel wool and then applied several more coats of French polish (allowing each coat to dry) until I felt the finish had enough 'body'. Finally, I put the

chair aside for a week or two for the finish to become fully hard and then rubbed it down along the grain with fine steel wool lubricated with wax polish. A brisk burnishing with a lint-free duster brought it up to a hard-wearing finish with a soft glow.

CUTTING LIST

	INCHES			MM		
	L	W	T	L	W	T
Part						
A 2 backfeet from						
1 piece	34½	7¼	1⅝	876	184	42
B 2 front legs	18	1⅞	1⅝	457	48	42
C 1 front rail	20½	3⅛	1¼	521	80	32
D 2 side rails	17¾	3⅛	1¼	451	80	32
E 1 back rail	15¼	3⅛	1¼	387	80	32
F 1 top back rail	16⅞	2½	1¼	429	64	32
G 1 back rail	15⅛	2	1	384	51	25
H 1 centre splat	13	3	½	330	76	12
J 2 side splats	13	1⅜	½	330	35	12
K 2 arm stumps	13¼	4¼	1¼	336	108	32
L 2 arms	16½	4¼	1¼	419	108	32
M 4 seat brackets	4½	4¼	1¼	115	108	32
Drop-in seat frame						
N 1 rail	17½	2¾	¾	445	70	19
O 1 rail	12¾	2¾	¾	324	70	19
P 2 rails	15¾	2¾	¾	400	70	19

Working allowances have been made to lengths and widths; thicknesses are net.

LADDERBACK CHAIR

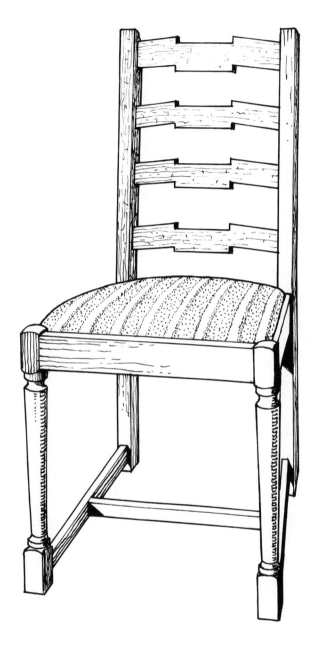

This is a simple design in softwood, planned for economy in cost, and to give a touch of a bygone age. Natural-finished pine furniture is finding a place within the home, and this type of chair can be made in sets, or as a one-off for use in the hall or bedroom.

GENERAL REMARKS

Chairs for domestic use can be constructed satisfactorily in softwood if the following points are observed. When designing, the sections of the components should be slightly increased as compared to those which would be used for hardwood; this reduces any weakening of the timber at the joints. Be careful to plot the joints so that too much material is not cut away by a mortise, bearing in mind that the tenon must be strong enough to do its job. Also, keep the work under pressure in the cramps until the

adhesive has fully set. Corner brackets should be diagonally grained in hardwood, and they should be fitted, well glued, and screwed in place. In this design, the plywood seat unit is also screwed in through corner brackets to increase its diagonal rigidity. If all these points are observed, there is every chance of success.

CONSTRUCTION

For the back legs choose timber that is free from cracks or weakening knots; while careful selection of material for these parts is important, some knots in other parts can enhance the appearance. Remember that extra length on the front leg blanks will be required for mounting in the lathe. A ⅜in chisel is suitable for all the mortise work, whether it is done by hand or machine.

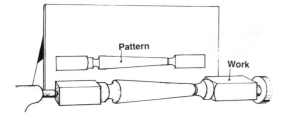

Fig. 14.1. A full-sized drawing is positioned behind the lathe for quick reference.

PARALLEL SIDES

The cutting list gives dimensions for a chair with parallel sides to its seat, but if the seat is required to diminish towards the back, some parts will have to be shortened, and a full size drawing of the setting-out will also be needed to obtain the necessary angles. A reduction of about 1in at each side would be suitable, but a beginner could make the chair with parallel sides for which a setting-out drawing is not fully essential.

TURNING THE LEGS

Make these first if there is any doubt whether the drawing can be followed accurately on this operation. The long tapered section of the leg should be made slightly swelled to add to the appearance, and it is actually easier to turn it to this shape. Take care to keep the legs clean after turning, and wrap them in paper to prevent discolouration if they are not to be used immediately.

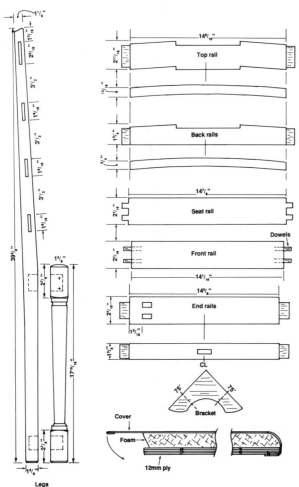

Fig. 14.2. Guide to the setting out and shaping of the various parts. The measurements are for a chair with parallel sides.

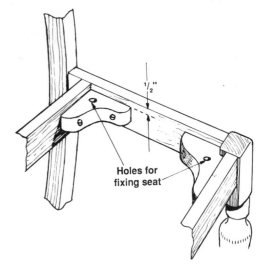

Fig. 14.3. Showing the corner brackets in place, ½in below the edge of the seat rail. Note holes bored for securing the upholstered unit.

ORDER OF ASSEMBLY

The ends of the chair should be glued up first and allowed to set, as the front rail is dowelled into the leg. The dowels extend into the tenons of the side rails and pierce them, so pegging the joint. Use ⅜in dia hardwood dowels.

FINISHING

As with all natural-finished woodwork, the final cleaning up is important. The sealing can be clear (white) French polish, or polyurethane varnish. This should be applied as soon as possible after the cleaning-up operation to preserve the natural colour as much as possible.

UPHOLSTERY

The most simple method is to build up on a ½in thick ply board with 1in chip foam. If the foam is undercut at the edges, clean rounded edges will result when the material is pulled taut. The completed seat unit must be secured with screws when the polishing operation has been completed.

CUTTING LIST

	INCHES			MM		
	L	W	T	L	W	T
2 back legs	39⅞	2¾	1⅛	1013	70	28
2 front legs	18⅜	1⅞	1⅝	467	48	42
1 top back rail	17	2⅞	1¼	432	73	32
3 back rails	17	2	1⅛	432	51	28
1 seat rail	16¾	2¾	⅞	425	70	22
1 front rail	14½	2¾	⅞	368	70	22
2 end rails	16⅞	2¾	⅞	429	70	22
2 side underframe rails	16⅞	1⅝	⅞	429	42	22
1 centre underframe rail	16¾	1⅝	⅞	425	42	22
1 piece for seat brackets	12	2¼	1	305	58	25
1 seat board, ply	15	12⅞	½	381	327	12

Also required: 1 piece chip foam 15in×13in×1in (381mm× 330mm×25mm); 1 piece cover fabric 21in×19in (535mm× 482mm).

Working allowances have been made to lengths and widths; thicknesses are net.

54

WRITING CHAIR

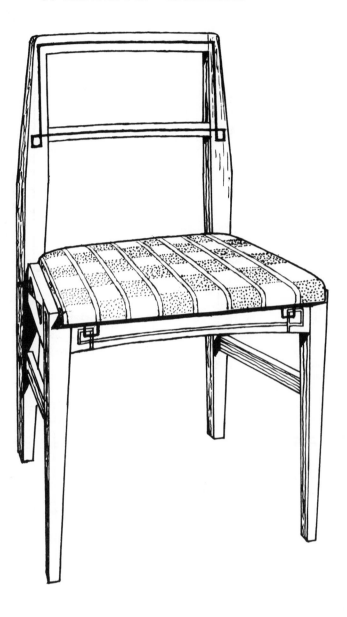

This chair is made of ash, veneered cross-grain fashion in walnut, but you can use other suitable hardwoods instead. The seat and back rails are inlaid with boxwood and ebony lines, and with satinwood squares. The seat, which is square in plan, consists of plastic foam on a webbed frame which rests on corner braces and on the front rail.

CONSTRUCTION
Fig. 15.1 shows the principal dimensions and construction, and it's worthwhile making a full-size drawing on a sheet of hardboard or plywood. Note that, to allow for rounding the corners at the tops of

all the legs, it is necessary to glue in pieces of walnut as shown in Fig. 15.3.

Work the back legs to the shape shown in the side elevation and mark the mortises on all the legs; Fig. 15.3 shows the arrangement of the joints for the front legs. The mortises on the back legs for the back and side rails meet so that the tenons touch inside. When all the mortising has been done, complete the shaping of the back legs as seen in the front elevation, Figs. 15.1 and 15.2; shape the front legs as well. Cut the tenons on all rails, fit each joint separately and put on identification marks where they will not be covered up later by the veneer. Test-assemble and cramp up the whole chair dry to ensure that all joints fit.

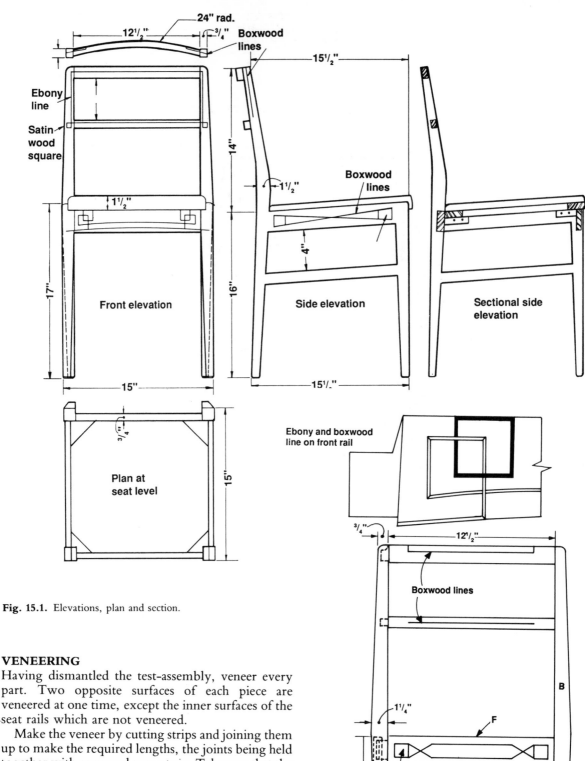

Fig. 15.1. Elevations, plan and section.

VENEERING

Having dismantled the test-assembly, veneer every part. Two opposite surfaces of each piece are veneered at one time, except the inner surfaces of the seat rails which are not veneered.

Make the veneer by cutting strips and joining them up to make the required lengths, the joints being held together with gummed paper tape. Take care that the width of the strips is a little larger than the wood on which they are to be glued so that when the glue has hardened you can trim the edges of the veneer level with the wood and continue with veneering the two remaining surfaces. You can use lengths of wood as cauls with paper or polythene film between them and the veneer to prevent their sticking to the veneer if there is any leakage of glue – G cramps will keep the cauls in place until the glue has set.

INLAYING

When you have completed all the veneering, you can mark out and cut the inlaid design with a cutting gauge and chisel; you can then glue the boxwood and ebony lines and the satinwood squares in place. Clean up with glasspaper, and polish every part before assembly.

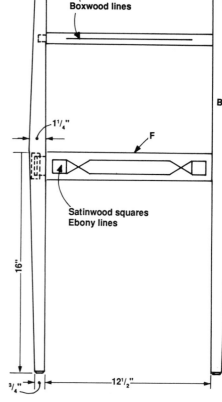

Fig. 15.2. Details of inlaid lines and squares.

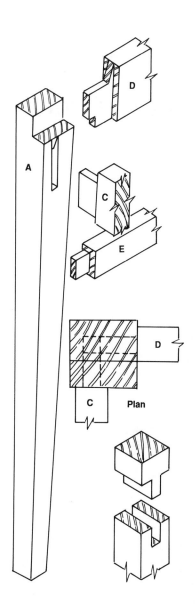

ASSEMBLY

You can now glue and cramp up the back legs and rails, and the front legs and rails as two separate sub-assemblies. When the glue has set, join them by means of the side rails, and glue and screw corner braces into the corners.

Make the seat frame by joining four pieces of wood together with halved corner joints, or by dowelling or tenoning. Next, tack the webbing on one side of the frame first and pull it tightly before tacking it on the opposite side. Cut the plastic or latex foam to size and attach the cloth upholstery by tacking it on the underside of the frame. Finally, bore a hole in the middle of the top edge of the front rail – this should accept a dowel glued to the seat frame which holds the seat in place.

CUTTING LIST

Part	INCHES			MM		
	L	W	T	L	W	T
A 2 front legs	18	1½	1¼	457	38	32
B 2 backfeet	31	ex 2¼	1¼	787	ex 58	32
C 1 front seat rail	15	2¼	⅝	381	58	16
D 2 side seat rails	15	2¼	⅝	381	58	16
E 2 underframe rails	15	1¼	⅝	381	32	16
F 1 back seat rail	15	2¼	¾	381	58	19
1 top back rail	14	1¼	ex 1½	356	32	ex 38
1 back stay rail	14	1	ex 1½	356	25	ex 38
4 seat frame rails	15	2	¾	381	51	19

Working allowances have been made to lengths and widths; thicknesses are net.

Fig. 15.3. Details of joints, and plan of leg fitting. The block which is glued in for rounding off the top of each leg is shown at bottom of illustration.

WINDSOR STICK-BACK CHAIR

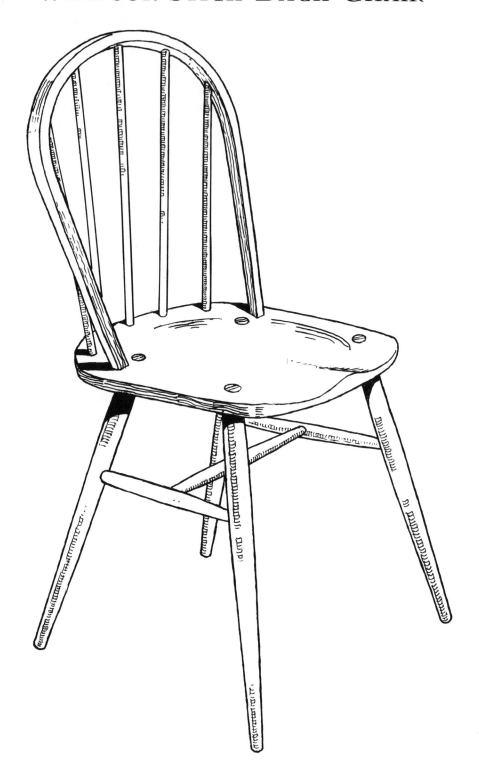

This Windsor chair has been designed to overcome some of the disadvantages of the traditional construction where the strength depends almost entirely on the seat. Normally, the holes for the legs, the back bow and the back dowels are sources of weakness, particularly at the back where the holes are necessarily close together. Obviously the seat must not split, and this is one reason why elm is chosen (another reason is that elm is one of the few trees that can yield wide enough pieces for the seat to be sawn out whole) and, although it is an attractive timber, it has a reputation for warping and twisting.

Plywood has been chosen for the seat of this chair as by its nature it will not split, is unlikely to

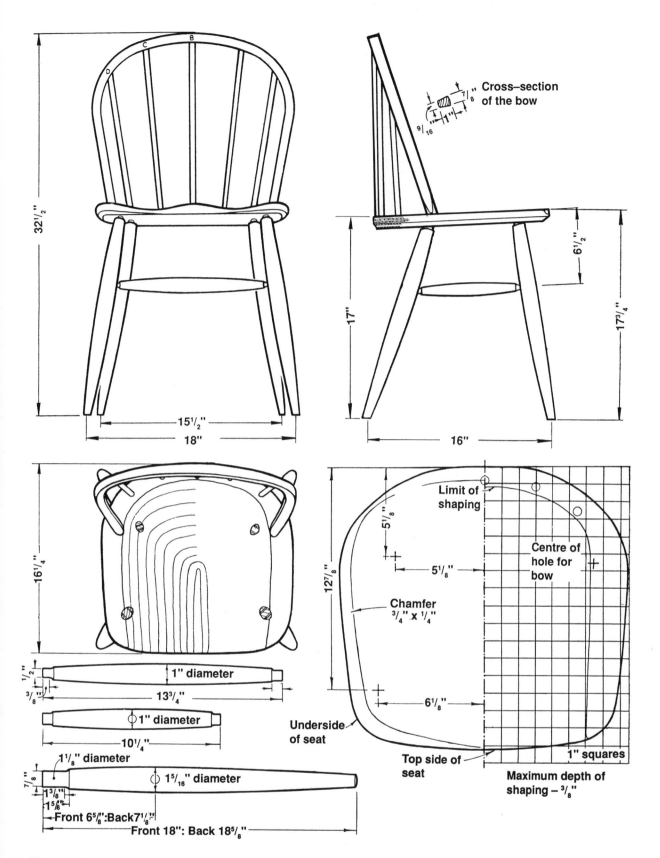

Fig. 16.1. Front and side elevations, with plan; also, dimensions for the seat and legs.

warp, and enables a considerably thinner seat to be used, with a consequent reduction in weight. Until recently, such a seat would have been difficult to shape by traditional cutting tools, but the new rasps and shaper tools with detachable blades make the hollowing out a straightforward job. If done carefully, the contours of the plies revealed by the hollowing make the seat look attractive and interesting.

HOLE DRILLING

Drill the holes for the legs before shaping the seat in any way. Study the plan view and you will see that the ends of the legs have their centres level with the front or back of the seat, although the back legs are slightly inside the seat and the front legs slightly outside it.

Mark the position of the holes according to the dimensions given in Fig. 16.1; remembering that the

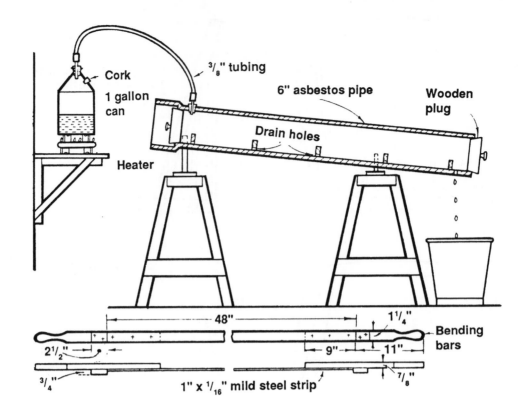

Fig. 16.2. Steaming box and bending apparatus.

holes for the back are marked on the opposite surface to the legs. Cramp the seat in the vice with the centre line vertical, with a short length of 2in by 1in batten cramped behind the hole centres to prevent splitting when the bit emerges from the seat. Fix a ⅞in bit in a carpenter's brace and mark the brace with a piece of chalk a distance from the end of the bit equal to the length of the leg. If this mark is correctly positioned in relation to the sides of the seat blank, it follows that the angle will be correct. The chalk mark should therefore be on a horizontal level with the edge of the plywood sheet and offset sideways.

The method of obtaining the sideways offset is shown in Fig. 16.5. Sight the chalk mark with the mark on the batten and get a helper to sight the horizontal level. Drill the holes for the back by a similar method but from the other side.

TABLE OF OFFSETS
(measured from 16¾in by 16¾in plywood)
Front legs .... ⅝in;
Back legs .... ⅝in;
Back .... zero at 9in from ends.

Mark the outline of the seat using the 1in squares marked on the drawing as a guide and cut it out to shape with a bandsaw, a sabre saw, or a fine-toothed bow saw. Temporarily fill the holes with softwood plugs and hollow the seat with an appropriate shaper tool, which should have a curved, toothed blade.

Finish the seat with glasspaper wrapped round a suitably shaped cork or wooden block, or with a power drill fitted with a flexible circular sanding disc; the front edge is best chamfered off by hand.

TURNING
Turn the legs from 1½in square beech or ash. This part of the job should be quite straightforward, but note that the shoulders must be rounded. Gauge the ⅞in diameter by trying each leg for size in a ⅞in hole

drilled in a piece of scrap wood, as carpenter's bits rarely drill exactly to size. The back legs are ⅝in longer than the front so that, when assembled, the seat should have a ¾in slope from front to back. Drill the ½in holes for the spindles by assembling the seat and the legs and aligning the bit according to the marks on the legs.

BENDING AND STEAMING THE BOW
It is important to cut the bow from 1in square straight grained ash or beech. Make the former as shown in Fig. 16.3 and fix it, mounted on a baseboard, to a suitable bench. Also make up the bending strap shown in Figs. 16.2 and 16.4.

Steam the bow for about 30 minutes in the apparatus shown in Fig. 16.2, which is based on a 48in by 6in dia asbestos pipe (readily obtainable from builders' merchants). Put on a pair of stout gloves as the wood will be hot, remove it and quickly place it between the end stops of the bending bar. With as little delay as possible fit the bow squarely into the moulding jig and pull it into shape. Quickly lock it with the locking bar shown in Fig. 16.4, or utilise a suitable sash cramp or even tie the ends with rope. Leave the bow in this position for 24 hours to set. Then remove it and shape it to the cross section shown in the side elevation in Fig. 16.1, rounding the ends to a good fit in the seat holes.

ASSEMBLING THE BACK
Mark the distances (BC) as 4in, and (CD) as 3¾in, on the inside of the bow by means of dividers, and then mark the positions of the supporting back dowels on the seat.

Align a ratchet brace and bit with the dowel marks and bore shallow holes for the dowels; the latter should be beech or birch. As the holes are shallow, you need not worry about any slight misalignment; you could use a power drill, with possibly a danger

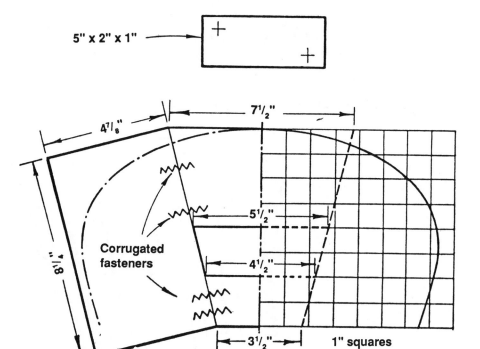

Fig. 16.3. Method for constructing the former.

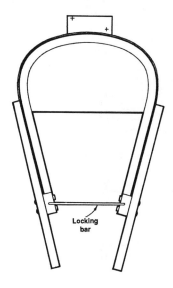

Fig. 16.4. After steaming, the bow is locked into position around the former.

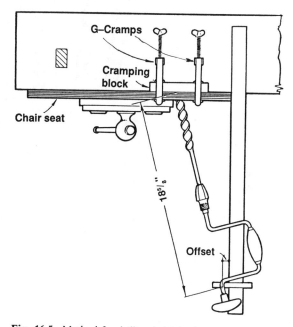

Fig. 16.5. Method for drilling holes in the seat at correct angles.

of some loss in accuracy of alignment but a gain in convenience. You can now insert the back dowels in place in the bow, and glue and then polish both the bow and the dowels.

FINAL ASSEMBLY AND POLISHING
You will find it more convenient if the legs and underside of the seat are polished before gluing. After gluing and wedging the legs in place, clean off the tops of the legs and polish the top surface of the seat. Next, glue the back sub-assembly in position and trim off any waste on the underside when the glue has set. Give the job a final polish and trim the legs for level if necessary.

As this type of chair is used either as a kitchen or a dining chair and is therefore subject to domestic accidents, you will find that a transparent water-resistant plastic lacquer is ideal, and it should be used in accordance with the manufacturer's instructions.

CUTTING LIST

	INCHES			MM		
	L	W	T	L	W	T
1 seat, birch ply	16¾	17	1	425	432	25
2 back legs	19¼	1½ sq		489	38 sq	
2 front legs	18½	1½ sq		470	38 sq	
2 side underframe spars	10¾	1¼ sq		272	32 sq	
1 cross underframe spar	14¼	1¼ sq		362	32 sq	
1 back bow	48	1 sq		1219	25 sq	
dowels for back out of	84	½ sq		2132	12 sq	

Working allowances have been made to lengths and to the square blanks for turning; thicknesses are net.

Farmhouse Kitchen Chair

This type of chair has, within the last few years, become almost a collectors' item along with other Victoriana. Fifteen or twenty years ago it was the exception rather than the rule not to find one in a Lincolnshire farmhouse kitchen. As the kitchen was the focal point of the domestic domain, the chair was generally known as 'Dad's' chair, and was usually accompanied by up to half a dozen matching brothers of the armless type which the remainder of the family used.

Although perhaps not particularly elegant by some standards, such chairs were functional and looked right in their setting. With the seat and back furnished with suitable cushioning, they were surprisingly comfortable, serving the double purpose of a carving chair, and one in which the farmer could take his ease and perhaps read the weekly newspaper after a long day's work in the fields. From when I was a boy, I can remember my father using one for over forty years, and it is still being used by his grandson! Certainly they could stand a lot of wear and tear without failing under the strain of often being used for purposes for which they were not originally intended!

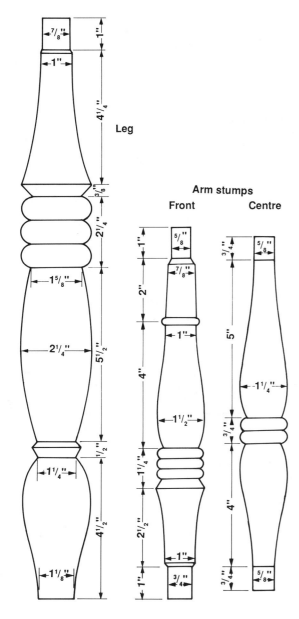

Fig. 17.1. Patterns and dimensions of legs and arm stumps.

Reproducing the chair today would not be a difficult job for the average woodworker who is equipped with a lathe that can accept 24 inches between centres. Admittedly, some simple steaming and bending of the top back rail and splats would be required; this, though, would not be difficult to improvise successfully and is described in Fig. 16.2, Design No 16.

The seat, being the main part around which the chair is built, could be termed the 'heart' of the job, and you may have to do a little searching to find just the right piece for it. What you should look for is a 20in square piece of 1½in thick stuff, which must be free from wind, have no sapwood in it, and preferably be completely knot free (although the odd small tight knot can be disregarded); above all, it should be free from even the smallest crack or split.

Little need be said about the construction; no difficulties should be encountered that a little thought and commonsense will not solve. Take it in stages, starting with the seat and legs, and complete the underframing first. It the seat is squared off before any shaping is done it will be much easier to mark out the positions of all the holes required in it before going any further.

For the legs you will need some good dry sound stuff not less than 2⅜in square; you will find that the arms can just be got from 3in by 1½in stuff. The back parts and stretchers need not necessarily be of beech, as ash would be suitable and is also a first class bending timber.

The outer back uprights should be cut from the solid, arranging the grain to favour the curve. It is difficult to give the exact lengths of the splats, and the dimension of each is best taken individually from the job after the frame has been knocked up dry. A generous length has been shown on the drawing which will doubtless need reducing when fitting. A good firm fit of all dowels and tenons should be

From one chair to the next, the designs varied only in minor details. Recently, in Derbyshire, I came across an armless example which differed only in that small half-round arches were cut in the lower edge of the top splats – a decorative detail I had not seen before.

The example shown was brought to me to have a new back leg put in, the reason being that one leg had got a particularly virulent attack of woodworm. Rarely have I seen a piece of wood in such a state. It literally crumbled away when taken out, but the extraordinary thing was that, apart from slight infestation of the two adjoining stretchers where they entered the leg, not one single worm hole could be found in any other part of the chair. Additionally, every glued joint was as sound as the day it was made, proof of the maker's ability and the use of well seasoned timber.

Generally these chairs were made of elm and beech stained a mahogany colour. Often at some time in their life they were freshened up with varnish stain – usually with dire results! This chair was no exception, the seat, legs, and arms being in elm with the leg stretchers and back parts in beech.

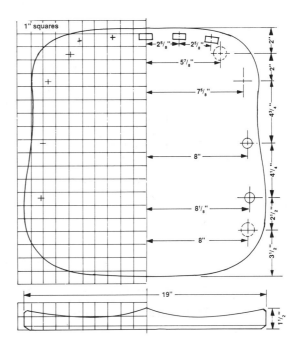

Fig. 17.2. One-inch grid drawing of seat plan; also, front edge profile.

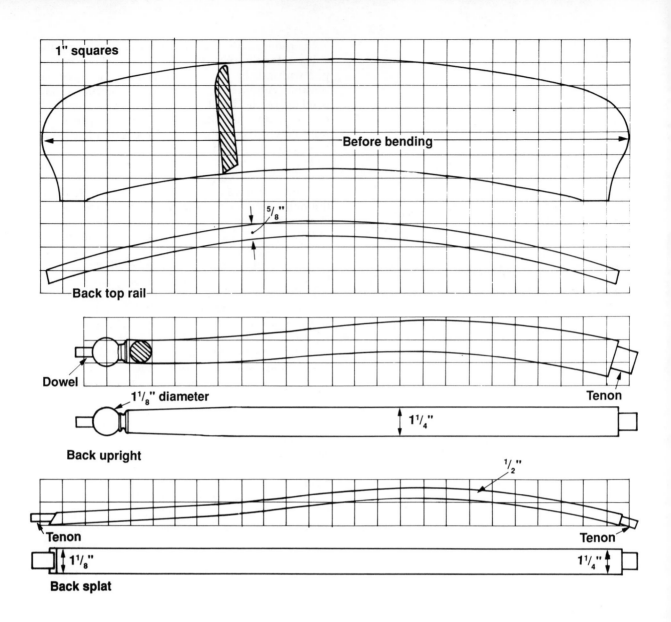

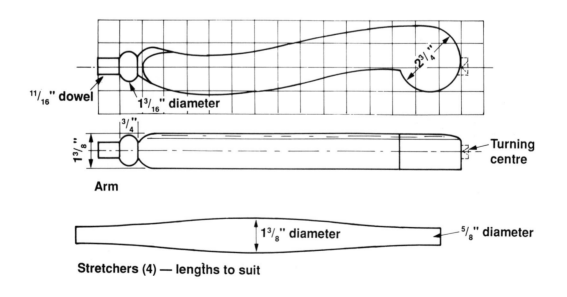

Fig. 17.3. One-inch grid drawing of shaped parts; also, details of stretcher.

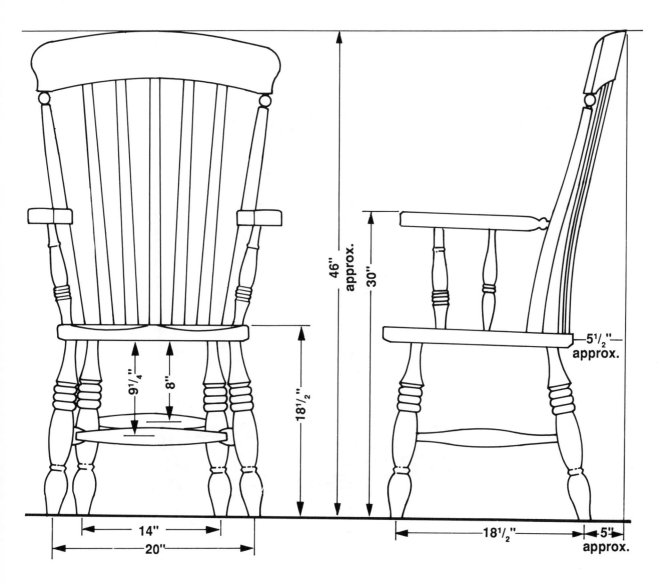

Fig. 17.4. Front and side elevations with principal dimensions.

aimed at, but lasting success with these joints depends very largely on the moisture content at the time of fitting – so have your timber dry!

As to staining – that is up to you. Personally I dislike staining any wood, my argument being that if you want an article 'red' make it in a red wood and if you want it 'brown' use a brown wood, and so on.

If you must stain, I would recommend a water stain, after first dampening the chair all over with water to raise the grain, and then glasspapering it down. Three of four thin coats of a matt polyurethane lacquer applied and then rubbed down with fine steel wool and wax and finally well burnished with a dry cloth will give an attractive and durable finish.

CUTTING LIST

	INCHES			MM		
	L	W	T	L	W	T
1 seat	20	20	1½	508	508	38
4 legs	19	2⅜ to 2¼ dia		483	60 to 57	
4 stretchers, lengths measured from job		1⅝ to 1⅜ dia			42 to 35	
2 back uprights	25	3¼	1¼	635	83	32
1 top rail, before bending	27	¾	⅝	686	19	16
2 arms	17	3⅛	1⅜	431	80	35
2 front stumps	12¼	1¾ to 1½ dia		311	45 to 38	
2 centre stumps	11¾	1½ to 1¼ dia		298	38 to 32	
5 back splats	27	2	½	686	51	12

Working allowances have been made to lengths and widths; thicknesses are net.

DINING CHAIR WITH DROP-IN SEAT

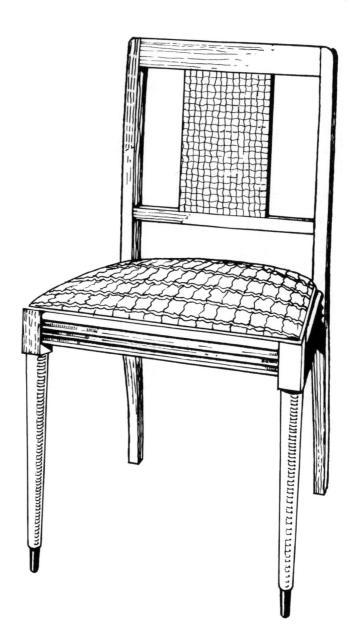

This handsome chair has a drop-in seat and the back splat can be covered with a plastic laminate, although a thin cushion of plastic foam upholstered with a fabric to match the seat can easily be substituted.

BACK LEGS

You can make an appreciable economy in timber for the back legs by marking one adjacent to the other, in other words by 'nesting' one into the other. Cutting them by hand is a long job, and you'll save a lot of time and labour by cutting them on a bandsaw, or by getting a friend who has one to do it for you. It is even more advantageous to do so, as a bandsaw cuts dead square and the legs can therefore

be marked closer together than is practicable in hand sawing; also, you will be starting off with a perfectly square edge.

Cut out a template in hardboard so that both legs are alike. Make sure you leave a straight, vertical portion level with the seat rails so that the shoulders of the last-named can be square. It's a good idea to mark where the joint will be on to the template as a guide.

FRONT LEGS

These are made 1¾in square at the top, and you will have to be careful when centering them for turning because the round immediately beneath the square

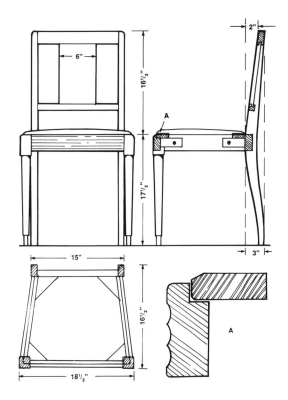

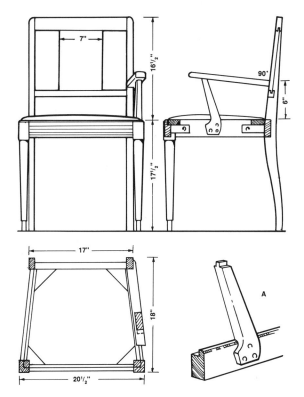

Fig. 18.1. Elevations and plan of small chair. Section at A shows detail at front seat rails.

Fig. 18.2. Elevations and plan of arm chair with detail of arm fixing at A.

almost runs out to the square faces. At the lower end the diameter is 1in with a ¾in diameter toe, and it can be in one piece, the toe being blacked-in when polishing.

SEAT FRAME

The mortises meet in the thickness of the legs, and, since the side tenons are cut parallel with the rails, their mortises have to be chopped at an angle which lines up with the rail angle. When you are chopping

Fig. 18.3. Exploded view of seat assembly.

these side mortises, mark the slope at the end of the leg as a guide to holding the chisel; alternatively you can set an adjustable bevel to the angle and place this to one side as a guide. It is, of course, necessary to set the mortise well down from the top so that it easily clears the rebate to be worked in the rails and leg tops to take the loose seat, and you can see this in Fig. 18.3.

The back rail has no rebate, and the mortises can therefore run the full width of the rail. Cut it in square, although the side rail must slope at a corresponding angle to those of the front legs.

The mid- and top rails of the back are tenoned in (Fig. 18.3); and both rails need a shallow mortise cut to receive the centre splat. Cut the shoulders in the wood normally, arranging the stub tenon so that the splat is set back sufficiently for the plastic laminate facing to stand in slightly; if you intend to upholster the splat you could adjust the tenon accordingly.

ASSEMBLING

Clean up all areas on the inner faces which cannot be dealt with later. The fluting of the seat rails is not essential and can be omitted if preferred, but it is an attractive decorative feature. Put the front and back together independently, testing not only for squareness and freedom from winding, but also to see that the leg faces are in alignment. Do this by placing a straightedge across the legs and seeing that the surfaces line up with it. The side rails are added after the adhesive has set.

The triangular seat brackets need to be thick (at least 1½in) to compensate for the fact that the chair has no underframing, and they should be individually fitted by gluing and screwing so that their top surfaces are level with the rebates. You will also need to continue these rebates by chopping them out on the tops of the front legs.

LOOSE SEAT AND UPHOLSTERY

Use plain halving joints, well-glued and screwed, for the loose seat frame. The assembled frame should be about ⅛in smaller all round than the seat frame into which it fits, so that there is a gap to accommodate the thickness of the cover fabric. Also, the top edges are given a wide chamfer, the bottom edges slightly taken off and all sharp corners removed to minimise the risk of the fabric being torn.

Fix down two webs in each direction on the seat;

then stitch hessian over the top. Position the stuffing material on top and hold it in place with one or two loops of twine tacked to the frame. Another piece of hessian is stretched over the whole and tacked to the underside so that the seat becomes nicely domed. Finally the covering is tacked over the whole.

CUTTING LIST

	INCHES			MM		
	L	W	T	L	W	T
2 back legs	35	3¼	1	889	83	25
2 front legs	20	2	1¾	508	51	5
1 front seat rail	18	2¾	1⅛	457	70	29

CUTTING LIST (continued)

	INCHES			MM		
	L	W	T	L	W	T
1 back seat rail	14½	2¾	1⅛	368	70	29
2 side seat rails	16	2¾	1⅛	407	70	29
1 back top rail	15	2¼	⅞	381	58	22
1 back top rail	15	1⅛	⅞	381	29	22
1 splat	11	6¼	⅝	279	159	16
3 loose seat rails	15	2¼	⅞	381	58	22
1 loose seat rail	18	2¼	⅞	457	58	22

Working allowances have been made to lengths and widths; thicknesses are net.

CONTEMPORARY STYLE DINING CHAIR

Before you begin to make any chair, it's advisable to draw a full-size plan and the front and side elevations on ply or hardboard and, in the case of this design, it's essential. Following the present trend in furniture, the chair is designed to combine lightness with comfort, and it is imperative to set out all the parts full size to get the correct slope of the back and the seat, upon which comfort depends.

MARKING OUT

Such a full-size drawing will enable you to work out the shoulder angles of the tenons, and to make and cut out a template for the backfeet. You will need a plank of 1¼in finished thickness timber for these, and by nesting one inside the other it is possible to cut more economically as although one leg requires a piece 3¾in wide, two can be cut from a 5½in width, allowing ample margin for sawing etc. The

front legs, the ladder back and the top rails also need 1¼in finished timber, and by working from a full-sized drawing you should find it easy to work out the necessary size of 1¼in plank for the number of chairs required.

BACKFEET

These taper from ¾in square at the top, reach a maximum of 1¼in thickness at the back seat rail, retaining this thickness for the 2in width of the rail, then tapering to ¾in at the foot. The maximum deviation in the side elevation is approximately 12½in from the top and, apart from this, all edges are straight; see Fig. 19.1.

RAILS

You can cut the ladder back rails from 1¼in stuff, locating them to finish flush with the front of the

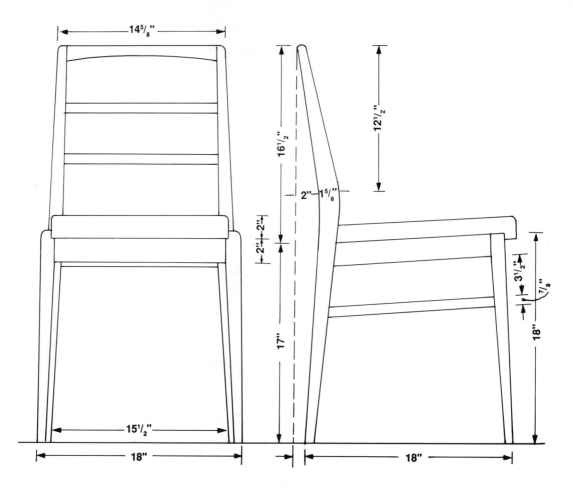

Fig. 19.1. Front and side elevations with principal dimensions.

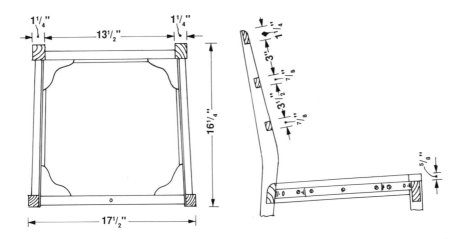

Fig. 19.2. Seat and back stay details.

chair back. Set the tenons of these rails as far back as possible, allowing a mere ¹⁄₁₆in shoulder at the back, and working them so that they run parallel with the face of the back rail. Note that owing to the set of the chair the shoulders will not be at right angles; you will have to plot this angle, and the angle on the face, from the full-size drawing.

You will see (Figs. 19.1 and 19.3) that the top rail is curved in plan as are the other two back rails, but it is also curved on the lower side elevation from 1¼in at the shoulders to ⁷⁄₈in at the centre. The tenons must be bevel – or slope – haunched so that

the joint will be hidden at the top when you cut the 'horns' from the backfeet.

Round off the back seat rail along the upper back edge; the inner edges finish flush with the backfeet. Work a ⁵⁄₈in by ¹⁄₈in rebate on the inner face of each of the side seat rails – this accepts the loose seat (Fig. 19.3). The rebate, of course, reduces the thickness of the rail at the top to ¾in; you can then slightly round off the outer top edge.

The life of the chair is largely governed by the strength of the joint between these rails and the backfeet, so the tenons should be as deep as possible

70

and carefully fitted to the mortises so that you achieve maximum strength.

The side stretcher rails also help to strengthen the chair so you should aim for the maximum tenoning area and an accurate fit to the mortises. Like the top seat rails, they are set back ³⁄₁₆in from the outside of the legs.

FRONT LEGS

The front legs taper from 1¼in square at the top to ¾in square at the bottom. Note that the rebate of the side rails is carried through at the top and that the front seat rail is inserted ⅝in lower, in line with the side rail rebate.

LOOSE SEAT AND SEAT SUPPORT BEARERS

The loose seat rests on four support blocks, so fit them accurately into the corners and then glue and screw them in place, using stout screws as the blocks contribute towards the strength of the chair.

As the rebate on the side rails is only ⅛in wide, it is advisable to fit seat support bearers to the sides and back, so that they can take much of the weight of the seat off the support blocks.

ASSEMBLY

Treat the back and front as separate units and glue and cramp them up, being careful that they are both

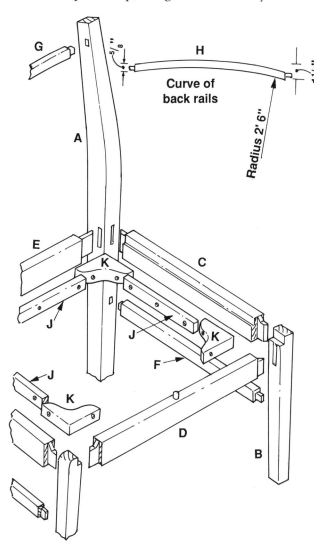

Fig. 19.3. Exploded view of assembly, and details of curved back rails.

dead square and out of winding. As there is no lower front rail, when you come to the cramping of the front seat rails and legs you must be sure that the final external measurement across the bottom of the legs is exactly 18in.

Allow the glue of these two sections to set thoroughly before you begin to glue and cramp up the side rails. Here, it is advisable to make a thin plywood template of the rake of the seat, so that you can maintain the correct angle at both sides. You can use a large sliding bevel instead but, owing to the slope of the back seat rail, you may find it awkward to achieve complete accuracy.

LOOSE SEAT FRAME

This projects by 1in over the front seat rail and you can make it from 2in by 1in softwood, to finish 1¾in by ⅞in. You can use hardwood but, if so, it should be one of the light hardwoods and one not liable to split, as considerable tacking has to be done later with heavy gauge tacks or clout nails to fix the webbing. You will find lapped joints at the corners, glued and screwed, quite sufficient; no useful purpose is served by mortising and tenoning the joints.

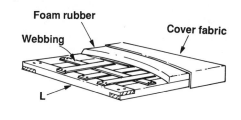

Fig. 19.4. Upholstery of seat.

Glue and screw the parts together, then plane the frame to fit, allowing a gap all round to accommodate the top fabric covering – test with a square piece of the cover at each side and at the back, as the seat should be a tight fit in the chair. The slight inward slope of the back seat rail will tend to prevent movement of the seat provided it is reasonably accurately fitted.

Insert and glue in a ⅜in dowel into the top of the front seat rail and make it of such a length that it protrudes by about ½in and locates into a ⅜in wide rectangular recess on the underside of the loose seat. This is better than boring a ⅜in round hole, as it is easier to cut and nail the fabric to fit a rectangular recess rather than a round hole.

UPHOLSTERING

The chair is designed to utilise resilient rubber webbing, and latex or plastic foam cushion seating. Although you can use traditional upholstery methods, the following is an easier and more effective method of working.

Space two strips of 1½in resilient rubber webbing from front to back and three from side to side, spacing them at regular intervals and interlacing them. Tack one end of each of the pieces of webbing on the top surface of the seat frame, using ½in clout nails or ⅝in upholstery tacks, making sure the tacks are at least ¼in away from the edges of the webbing. Next lay the open end of the webbing over the opposite rail and, without stretching, mark the inner edge of the rail on to it. From this mark make another one which is at a distance 10% less (if the original distance was 18in, then deduct 1.8in – say 2in) – so that the second mark gives a length of 16in.

Stretch the webbing until the second mark is in line with the inside edge of the seat frame, tack it down and cut off the waste. Continue with each piece in the same manner.

The latex or plastic foam cushion for the seat should be good quality and of medium to high density. Cut the foam accurately to fit the top of the seat frame and leave the edges square and not rounded off, as it is preferable for the appearance of the chair for the seat cushion to have a square-edged effect. You can stick the foam down with a few dabs of upholstery adhesive to prevent movement.

SEAT COVER

This is laid over the foam cushion, and a hem is turned in at the back and tacked to the underside of the loose seat. Work round the seat without pulling the fabric tight, as any tension will cause the cushion to assume a domed shape and this gives an undesirable effect. The corners are formed in the usual way so that the lapped joint is seen from the side only, allowing the front line to appear unbroken. You can use a small touch of upholstery adhesive to make this joint more stable, but it's not essential. A piece of material should be hem-tacked on top of the fabric

covering on the underside of the seat to give a neat finish and keep out dust.

All wooden edges should be slightly rounded before polishing.

CUTTING LIST

	INCHES			MM		
	L	W	T	L	W	T
Part						
A 2 backfeet	34	3¾	1¼	863	95	32
B 2 front legs	19	1⅜	1¼	483	35	32
C 2 side seat rails	16½	2⅛	⅞	419	54	22
D 1 front seat rail	18	2⅛	⅞	457	54	22
E 1 back seat rail	16	2⅛	⅞	407	54	22
F 2 side stretcher rails	17	1	¾	432	25	19
G 2 ladderback rails	15½	1	1¼	394	25	32
H 1 top back rail	15	1⅜	1¼	381	35	32
J 3 seat bearers	8½	1	½	216	25	12
K 4 seat blocks	3¼	3¼	⅞	83	83	22
L 4 seat frame battens	16½	2	⅞	419	51	22

Also required: 72 in (1828 mm) of 1½in (38mm) resilient rubber webbing; 1 piece cover fabric 22in (559mm) square; 1 piece plastic or latex foam 16in (407mm) square.
Working allowances have been made to lengths and widths; thicknesses are net.

Dining Chair with Laminated Bends

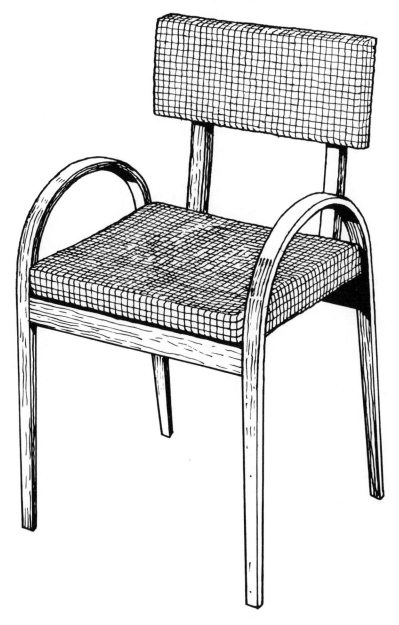

This dining chair is easily made and uses steam bending and laminating techniques: only ¼in and ⅜in thicknesses of wood are used in the bends. It contains only eight mortise and tenon joints; the result is pleasing and the chair is fascinating to make.

The leg/arm frames are laminated in three layers, the outer ones being of oak and the inner one, Burmese teak; allow an extra 6in or so before bending. The bent back supports are made similarly except that only a ¼in thickness is required in the teak.

CONSTRUCTION

The front and back rails are tenoned into the leg/arm frames with 1⅛in by ¼in tenons, and the seat rails are shaped as illustrated and tenoned into the front and back rails. A through ⅜in tenon is suitable and can be wedged to give maximum strength and an added decorative feature if contrasting wood is used.

You can make the back rest of solid oak and screw it with brass screws to the front of the back supports, and its edges can be chamfered. As an alternative, use plywood.

The seat is formed by five dowels drilled into the seat portion of the back supports, the centres being 2in apart (measured from the inside edge of the front rail). The back supports are then notched into the back rail and screwed to the inside edge of the seat rails with three brass screws.

BENDING PROCESS

Make a former of ⅜in ply and cut it to shape for the leg/arm frames. The semi-circular curved portion is built up to 1¼in thick by screwing and gluing pieces of softwood where required. You could use 1¼in by ⅞in solid oak for these parts, but the oak and the Burmese teak give an alternative and attractive effect.

Steaming is for half an hour in a steam chest. As

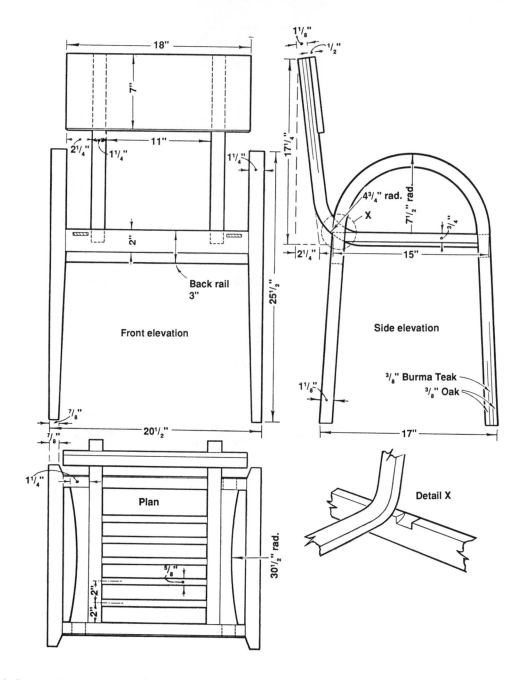

Fig. 20.1. Front and side elevations, and plan. Detail X shows how the back supports are notched into the back rail.

you do not need to steam the complete length of the laminates you can make an open-ended chest (already described in Fig. 16.2, Design 16), long enough to accommodate the section to be bent, and with its ends blocked with damp newspaper or rag. When taken out – the teak being in the middle – the outer oak strip should be G-cramped to the flexible metal band while the two inner strips are left free.

Bending these pieces is quite a simple matter; see Fig. 20.2. One sash cramp pulls in the two sides and another holds them in place until dry. Remove the assembly from the former, and wipe the teak over with a de-greasing agent so that glue will adhere to it.

Glue the inner edges and cramp the assembly back on to the former until the glue has set; G-cramps will again be required to hold the layers together. You will also need to line the base of the former with paper to stop the laminates sticking to it. Remove the glued assembly and work it to the required shape; the centre laminate of teak can be moulded round the edges with a scratch stock to give an attractive effect.

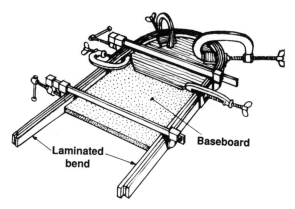

Fig. 20.2. Former for bending the side frames; it is used both for bending the wood to shape after steaming, and as a cramping jig for gluing up.

THE BENT BACK SUPPORTS

You will need to build another former (see Fig. 20.3) for these on ⅜in plywood, containing the correct angle for the bend. Parts (A), (B), and (D) are screwed into position on the baseboard, while (C) is free to move.

The wood for the bent back supports is steamed for half an hour. When you take it out after steaming, bend it slightly by hand and place it in the former with the ¼in teak lamination in the middle. Use a sash cramp to pull block (C) tightly on to the laminates and compress them into the requisite curved position. Then G-cramp the outer portions of the laminates to the blocks (B), and apply pressure evenly along the length.

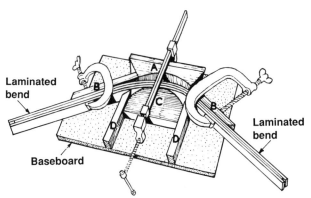

Fig. 20.3. Former for back supports. Pieces (A), (B), and (D) are screwed to the baseboard; (C) is free to be cramped against the inside of the bend.

Allow the assembly to dry out for half a day; then, after marking their exact position, remove the laminates from the former. Then glue the inside faces and put the assembly back into the bending jig. For more difficult or thicker strips, G-cramp a flexible metal strip to the outer edge of the first laminates. Allow the glue to set and remove from the jig and clean up, shaping and moulding the centre teak lamination with a scratch stock if required. You will find there will be no springing when the bent wood is taken from the jig after gluing.

The back rest can be screwed to the supports, the dowel holes drilled in the appropriate places, and the

seat part of the back rest supports screwed to the shaped seat outer rails. But before assembling this part of the chair, namely the back and seat, thoroughly clean them up and give them a priming coat of 50/50 plastic lacquer/thinners.

FINAL ASSEMBLY

The seat side rails which you have shaped and mortised into the front and back rails, and the front and back rails which have been mortised into the leg and arm rails, can now be glued up and the through tenons wedged, if desired. You can then give the completed chair its final coats of plastic lacquer.

CUSHION AND BACK REST

The cushion is made of plastic or latex foam 19in wide by 14½in deep by 2in thick, and the oak back rest is covered with 1½in thick matching foam; fix it in position with two material straps stitched to the covering material.

CUTTING LIST

	INCHES			MM		
	L	W	T	L	W	T
Leg and arm frames						
4 pieces, oak	66	1½	⅜	1676	38	10
2 pieces, teak	66	1½	⅜	1676	38	10
Back supports						
4 pieces, oak	36	1½	⅜	914	38	10
2 pieces, teak	36	1½	¼	914	38	6
Other parts in oak						
1 front rail	20	2¼	⅞	508	58	22
1 back rail	20	3¼	⅞	508	83	22
2 side rails	16	1½	¾	407	38	19
1 back rest						
(could be ply)	18½	7¼	½	470	185	12
5 seat dowels	12	⅝ dia		305	16 dia	

Generous allowances have been made for bending, and also to widths; thicknesses are net.

Dining Chairs with Upholstered Backs

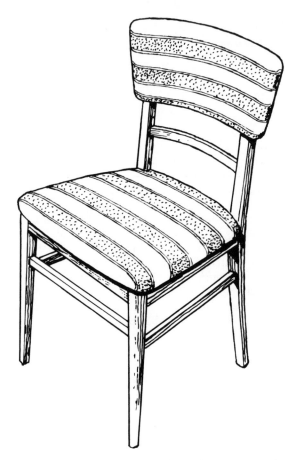

The sure sign of a good craftsman is the ability to make a strong, comfortable chair moulded to the body. The seat should be the right depth and height, the arms at a comfortable level, and the back with a correct rake for all requirements.

These designs will give you chairs that are both strong and light; arms to a dining chair are really unnecessary, but they look elegant on social occasions. You will find that beech or a similar hardwood is most suitable, with all edges nicely rounded off, the job being finished with white (clear) French polish.

FULL-SIZE DRAWINGS
Make full-size side and front elevation, and plan, drawings of each chair on hardboard or plywood before commencing the actual construction – the dimensional drawings in Figs. 21.1 and 21.2 will help

you here. These drawings will enable you to make economical use of timber by making templates of the backfeet, arms, and stumps, and nesting them.

GENERAL CONSTRUCTION
As is usual with most chairs, the backs and fronts are assembled as separate units, being afterwards connected by the side rails and stretchers, with the addition of the arms and supports in the case of arm chairs (also called 'carvers'). Fig. 21.3 shows the various joints which are identical for both the arm and small chairs.

Taper the front legs (A), Fig. 21.3 from beneath the seat rails on the inside faces, and work the mortises for the tenons of the front frame rail and the stretchers. You can then glue and cramp up the parts as a sub-assembly, rounding off the corners of the legs after the glue has set.

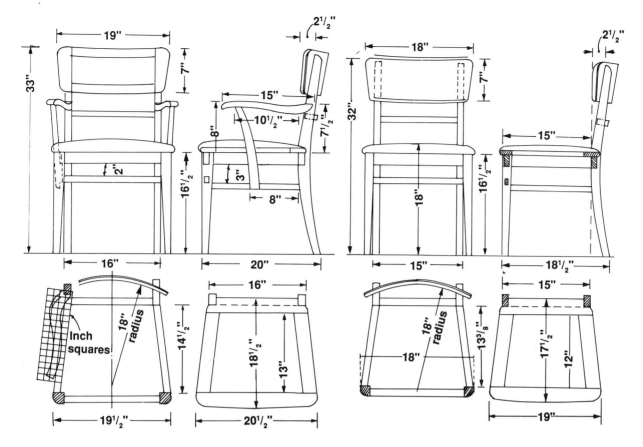

Fig. 21.1. Elevations, plans, and dimensions of arm chair.

Fig. 21.2. Elevations, plans, and dimensions of small chair.

Now start the back sub-assembly by sawing the backfeet, (D), to the shape of your previously-made template and cut the mortises for the tenons on the back frame rail and spandrail, the latter being cut to the swept radius shown in Fig. 21.2. Finally, glue and cramp up.

UPHOLSTERED BACKS

These can be made in several ways, the method shown being convenient if you have only limited facilities.

Use panels of 4mm thick plywood, making sure that the outer grain runs vertically for easy bending. Note that the corners and edges are rounded and the fronts faced with tacking pieces (P) and (Q) glued and pinned on from the rear. Saw the shaped strips from the solid or alternatively, three ³⁄₁₆in thick strips can be laminated together in a saddle, as shown in Fig. 21.3. Male and female moulds are cut from a single piece of scrap wood of sufficient thickness and are glued to the plywood, using the same mould for handscrewing together; wing pieces (P) are afterwards attached in the same manner.

You will need to pare away the backfeet as shown in Fig. 21.3 to accept the shaped back, which is screwed to them from the front. Plot the angled shoulders of the side frame rails from your full-size drawings. Insert the dowels at right angles to the shoulder faces – you'll find it easier to do this if you make a small drilling jig for the purpose. Make the dowels long enough to penetrate and peg the tenons of the front and back frame rails.

To obtain the shoulder lengths of the side stretcher rails, (N), assemble the seat frame dry and mark off from the legs.

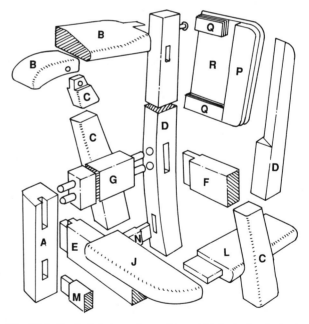

Fig. 21.3. Exploded view of assembly, which is similar for both chairs.

ARMS AND STUMPS

Shape these from the plotted plan in Fig. 21.1, noting that they are cut on two planes – in other words, a compound shape. Where they are joined to the backfeet, notch round the latter and screw the arms in from the rear, countersinking and plugging (or, better still, pelleting) the screw heads. Reinforce the joints by inserting hardwood dowels into the arms near the joints to provide extra grip for the screw threads.

The shaped arm stumps, (C), need to be eased away above the seat rails for the upholstered seat frame, as shown in Fig. 21.3. The stumps have an outward splay which will mean that you have to pare away the frame rails at an angle to allow for this. The stumps, (C), are carried down to the stretcher rails and notched over and screwed from inside. Peg the tenons that enter the underside of the arms with ¼in dia dowels; you will find that the appearance of the arms is greatly improved by dishing them on the upper surfaces (Fig. 21.3), and then rounding off both the arms and the stumps.

SEAT FRAMES

The upholstered seat frames are made in hardwood strongly mortised and tenoned together, and shaped to the back; round off all edges. When you come to notching the frame around the backfeet, don't forget to allow for the turn-over of the covering material – this should be carried well under the seat frame before fixing and screwing it up through the rails.

CUTTING LIST

	INCHES			MM		
	L	W	T	L	W	T
Part						
Small chair						
A 2 front legs	17	1⅞	1⅝	432	48	42
B 2 backfeet from						
1 piece	32½	6	1⅛	825	153	29
E 1 front frame rail	17¾	2¼	1⅛	451	58	29
F 1 back frame rail	15	2¼	1⅛	381	58	29
G 2 side frame rails	14½	2¼	1⅛	369	58	29
H 1 back stay	15	2¾	⅞	381	70	22

CUTTING LIST (continued)

	INCHES			MM		
	L	W	T	L	W	T
J 1 seat frame	19½	3	¾	495	76	19
K 1 seat frame	16½	3	¾	419	76	19
L 2 seat frames	15	2½	¾	381	64	19
M 1 front stretcher	17¾	1¼	⅝	451	32	16
N 2 side stretchers	16	1¼	⅝	407	32	16
P 2 tacking pieces	7½	3¼	⁹/₁₆	191	83	14
Q 6 pcs for 2 tacking						
pieces	14½	1¾	³/₁₆	369	45	5
R 1 back panel, ply	7½	20¼	4mm	191	515	4
Arm chair						
A 2 front legs	17	2	1¾	432	51	45
B 2 arms from 1 piece	15½	5¾	1⅜	394	147	35
C 2 stumps from						
1 piece	14½	4¾	1⅛	369	121	29
D 2 backfeet from						
1 piece	33½	6	1⅛	851	153	29
E 1 front frame rail	19	2¼	1⅛	483	58	29
F 1 back frame rail	16	2¼	1⅛	407	58	29
G 2 side frame rails	15½	2¼	1⅛	394	58	29
H 1 back stay	16	2¾	⅞	407	70	22
J 1 seat frame	21	3	¾	533	76	19
K 1 seat frame	17½	3	¾	445	76	19
L 2 seat frames	16	2½	¾	407	64	19
M 1 front stretcher	19	1¼	⅝	483	32	16
N 2 side stretchers	17	1¼	⅝	432	32	16
P 2 tacking pieces	7½	3¼	⁹/₁₆	191	83	14
Q 6 pcs for 2 tacking						
pieces	15½	1¾	³/₁₆	394	45	5
R 1 back panel, ply	7½	21¼	4mm	191	540	4

Working allowances have been made to lengths and widths; thicknesses are net.

CARVER DINING CHAIR

The main feature of the chair is the curved arms, which give the design its elegant and graceful appearance. The front rail and the top middle back rails have a slight curvature and, although the curve is not great enough for it to be essential to laminate them, you will find it good practice for the making of the more complex arms.

BACKFEET AND BACK SEAT RAIL
Make a template of the backfoot shape, which you can then use to mark out. Saw them out with a bandsaw, and leave at least 1in of waste on all ends.

Plane up the outside faces of the legs as face sides; then place the face sides together and screw the two backfeet to each other through the waste wood you have left on the tops and bottoms. Finally, clean them up to their finished shape with spokeshave and scraper.

Prepare the back seat rail next, and mark out and cut the twin mortise and tenon joints, as detailed in Fig. 22.2. Shape the backfeet on the inside faces, and fit and cramp up the joints (dry) to make up a basic back frame.

TOP AND MIDDLE BACK RAILS
These have a curvature of ⅞in their length, and you can either cut them out of the solid, or laminate them. If you choose the latter method, you will need

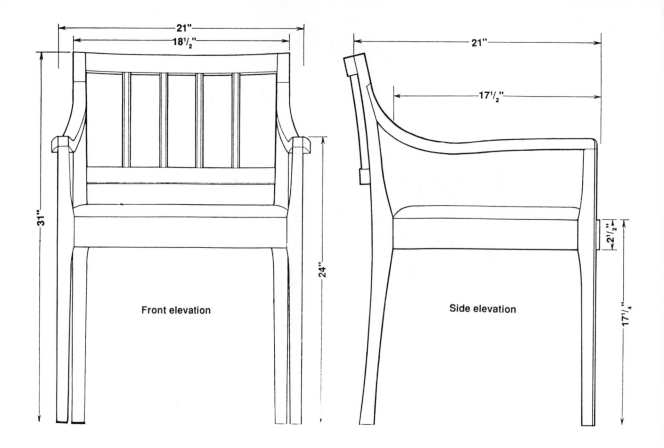

Fig. 22.1. Front and side elevations.

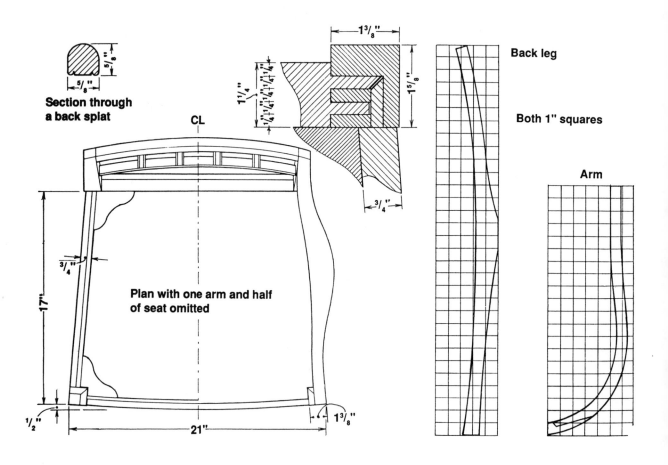

Fig. 22.2. Plan, with sections and plotted shapes.

a former made out of softwood. You will have to cut and plane the laminations and, if you have a planer blade which you can use on your circular saw, it should be a straightforward job.

When you have cleaned up the rails and planed them to size, cramp them into position with G-cramps on the front of the backfeet, which have already been assembled with the back seat rail as described above. Mark the shoulder lengths and angles on the rails, and set a sliding bevel to complete the marking of the shoulders. Make up a cramping block from scrap for the rails, so that you can gauge the tenons at right angles to the shoulders. Then make these joints, and assemble the chair back dry.

BACK SPLATS

Prepare these to a ⅝in square section before you shape them, and note that they follow the curve of the backfeet between the two back rails. Then cramp them into position on the assembled back, and mark the shoulders off. Mark out and cut the small ³⁄₁₆in stub tenon and mortise joints. Finally, shape the splats in section, working the channelling on the fronts with a scratch stock.

FRONT LEGS AND RAIL

The next step is to prepare the front legs to a 1⅜in square section, and mark the positions of the seat joints. As with the back rails, the front seat rail has a slight curvature. The advantage in laminating this rail is that it solves the problem of cutting a curved rebate, as the two inside laminations can be cut ½in narrower than the other four to form the rebate. Pin small blocks to the inside face of the former to ensure correct location. After you have laminated and cleaned up the rail, mark out and cut the mortise and tenon joints – these have ¼in tenons.

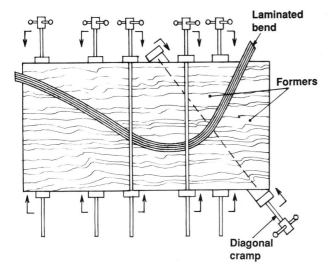

Fig. 22.3. Method for cramping laminations.

SIDE AND FRONT SEAT RAILS

Prepare these to 2½in by ¾in and then mark them out. It is worth making a full-size plan of the seat to obtain the correct angles of the shoulders and tongues of the tenons that enter the backfeet. Again, you can use a block to cramp to the rails, in order to get the tenons at right angles to the shoulders.

The joints into the front legs are quite straightfor-

ward, as the side rail meets the front leg at right angles. After cutting these joints and rebating the rails ½in by ¼in, you can test-assemble the whole chair, but without the arms, of course.

BACK AND FRONT ASSEMBLY

After dismantling the test-assembly, clean up the parts of the back frame with glasspaper, polish them (it is easier to do at this stage than when the complete chair is glued up and assembled), and glue and cramp them together.

Next shape the front legs and, after cleaning up and polishing, glue them together with the front rail.

ARMS

Make a template to the shape as drawn in Fig. 22.2, and make a softwood former, Fig. 22.3. The ⅛in laminations should easily follow round this shape without any soaking or steaming, but you will find that it is advisable to attach newspaper temporarily to both faces of the former before starting to glue up, otherwise the paper tends to slip out of position and the laminations may well end up glued to the former!

Cramp up the laminations as shown in Fig. 22.3 with the diagonal G-cramp applying pressure at right angles to the main curve. When you have glued up the arms, make a thin cardboard template of their plan shape from which you can then mark out and cut them roughly to shape.

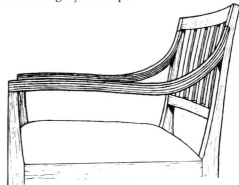

Fig. 22.4. Profile of arm shape, showing its joint with back leg.

Next, work the spliced shape on the arms where they meet the backfeet, Fig. 22.4, and then cramp them into position on the outside of the backfeet. Mark out the backfeet from the shape on the arms, and cut them to receive the arms.

When you have fitted these joints, test-fit the whole chair together with the side rails in position, dry, and mark the positions for the ¼in dowels for joining the arms both to the backfeet and to the tops of the front legs. Use two dowels for each back joint, and place one centrally in the top of each front leg for each front joint.

Now finally glue up the chair, and do the final shaping of the arms. Fit the seat corner blocks, and screw and glue them into position.

SEAT

This is simply a piece of ½in plywood cut to shape, covered in 1in thick plastic or latex foam, and upholstered. A slightly softer seat can be obtained by cutting out the centre of the plywood, and tacking rubber webbing across the hole before placing the foam over the top.

CUTTING LIST

	INCHES			MM		
	L	W	T	L	W	T
2 backfeet from						
1 piece	34	7	1⅜	863	178	35
2 front legs	24½	1⅝	1⅜	622	42	35
1 back seat rail	18½	2¾	1¼	470	70	32
1 top back rail:						
6 laminations, each	20	1¾	⅛	508	45	3
1 middle back rail,						
6 laminations, each	20	1½	⅛	508	38	3
4 back splats from						
1 piece	9½	4	⅝	242	102	16

CUTTING LIST (continued)

	INCHES			MM		
	L	W	T	L	W	T
1 front rail:						
6 laminations, each	21½	2¾	⅛	546	70	3
2 side rails	18½	2¾	¾	470	70	19
2 arms:						
14 laminations, each	24	2¾	⅛	609	70	3
4 corner blocks from						
1 piece	12	3½	1⅜	305	89	35
1 seat, plywood	20½	17	½	521	432	12

Working allowances have been made to lengths and widths; thicknesses are net.

CONTEMPORARY-STYLE CARVER CHAIR

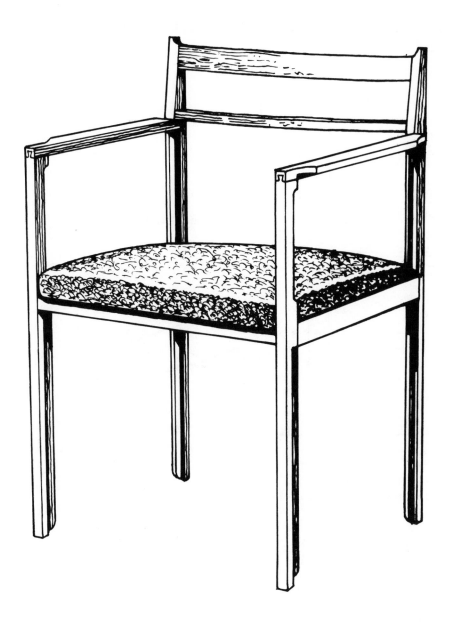

PREPARATION

Begin by preparing the wood for the two side frames. Mark out the joints, four for each frame, and from Figs. 23.1, 23.2, and 23.3 you will see the type of joint to be used. After marking, cut them all and have a test-assembly to see how they fit.

Next, mark out for the shaping. Most of the wood to be cut away can be removed at this stage, but do not try to get a final finish where one member meets another until after the final assembly and the adhesive has set.

WORKING THE REBATES

These run on the inner faces of the back legs and the lower part of the front legs (Figs. 23.1, 23.2, and 23.3). They are best worked with a powered router or spindle moulder but you can work them fairly

easily by hand methods using a rebate plane, bullnose plane, chisels, glasspaper, etc.

A rebate runs under each of the arms and is bevelled by using a rebate plane at a sloping angle – a wooden one is best for this job. The width of the rebate stops about 1/8in short of the leg thickness (see Figs. 23.1 and 23.1A) to give greater strength to the bridle joint at the back. The shaping in plan (Figs. 23.1 and 23.1A) can be worked with a bow- or coping saw and smoothed off.

THE LEGS

The upper front legs are simply a bow-saw and bullnose plane job, with help from a rasp and glasspaper (see Figs. 23.1 and 23.1A). Get a good finish here now because it does not have to meet with anything else.

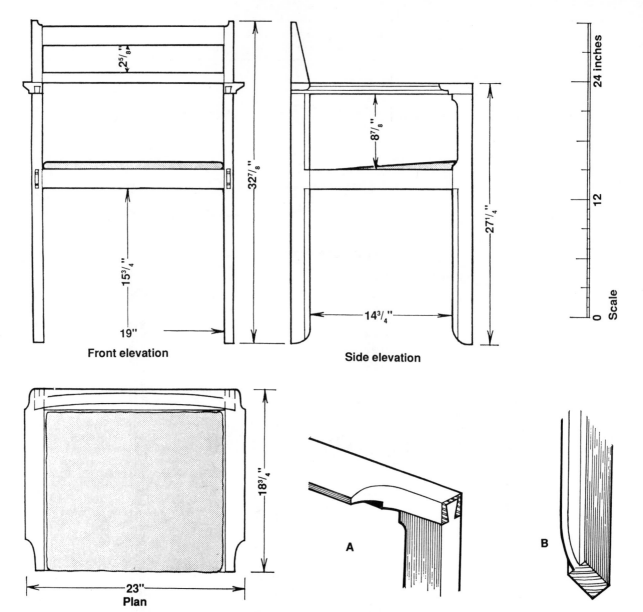

Fig. 23.1. Front and side elevations, and plan. The joint and shaping where the arm meets the leg are shown at A; detail at bottom of leg is shown at B.

The slope seen from the side on the tops of the back legs can be sawn and planed, and the convex detail at the very top sawn out and smoothed off.

ASSEMBLY

When all the shaping has been done, have another test-assembly and then glue and cramp up. Don't forget to cut the wedges for the tenons before gluing. Make sure the frames are absolutely flat during the time the adhesive is setting. When this has happened, finish off the detailing and apply a coat of polish; somewhat unconventionally, I experimented with teak oil, and have found that on beech it gives a soft, in-surface glow.

CROSS PIECES

There are six of these to prepare, all with a between-shoulder length of 19in, and the joints to be used are shown clearly in Figs. 23.2 and 23.3. Note that the dowels enter the legs only as far as the tenons and are not used to peg the tenons in position.

I completed the side frames almost entirely before marking out the positions for the joints to connect with the cross pieces. To do this afterwards is not so

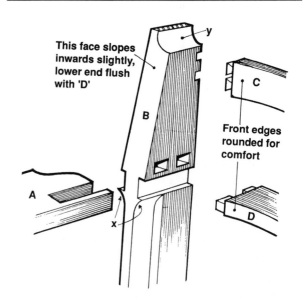

Fig. 23.2. Exploded view of joints at intersection of arm, leg, and back rails. Upper back rail, C, is jointed to leg B with twin lap-dovetails. Lower back rail, D, is jointed to B with twin stub tenons, and arm A is jointed to B with a bridle joint. The shaping X and Y is done roughly before jointing and finished after glueing.

difficult as it first appears, as the side frames are flat (apart from the arm projection) and this method does ensure similarity on both frames. But if you prefer to mark out and cut these joints before gluing the frames, all should go well.

Look at Fig. 23.3 and you will see that part (C) is secured with a housed dovetail and is screwed to (B) after assembly. The best way to mark the position for the socket for this dovetail is to cramp (B) into place, butt (C) against it and then mark round the previously-cut tail. (C) and (B) should be glued as well as screwed together. The treatment for all four corners is identical except for part (B) (Fig. 23.3) at the front of the chair, as this must be bevelled to support the base of the seat firmly.

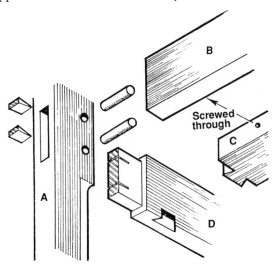

Fig. 23.3. Exploded view from below of joints used at junction of legs, side, and cross rails: this construction is used at all four corners. Side rail D is tenoned through back leg A and fixed with two wedges. Cross rail B is dowelled into A, and is on the same level as D. The dowels only enter A as far as the face of the tenon. Cross rail C is lap-dovetailed into the lower side of D. It butts against the side of B and is screwed through into it. You can screw C through the dovetail into D is required.

BACK RAILS

The jointing of these can easily be seen in Fig. 23.2 and its accompanying caption. You can certainly do quite a lot of shaping before gluing but try to leave some for later, as quite a small difference can affect comfort.

FINAL STAGES

Gluing, assembling, and cramping is simple – don't forget to check for squareness – but after removing the cramps you will come to an admittedly irksome bit, namely the final shaping of all meeting edges so that they run in exactly to meet each other. This is not a big job, but it's fiddling, and I consider it best left until this stage for perfect results. The bottoms of the legs (Fig. 23.1B) are also given a final trim at this stage to make the chair stand level.

THE SEAT

This is the last job of all. The simplest way to do it is to screw two fillets along the inside of the side rails, at an angle, and to make a drop-in seat which will be a push fit. I used some 1⅜in ply, covered with plastic foam and upholstered with two layers of fabric. There should be a few holes in the ply to allow the foam to 'breathe'.

CUTTING LIST

	INCHES			MM		
	L	W	T	L	W	T
2 backfeet	33¼	2	¾	844	51	19
2 front legs	27¾	2	¾	705	51	19
2 arms	18¾	2	¾	476	51	19
2 side rails	19¼	2	¾	489	51	19
6 cross members	20¾	2	¾	527	51	19
2 fillets	13	⅞	¼	330	22	6
1 seat, plywood	19½	17	⅜	495	432	10

Working allowances have been made to lengths and widths; thicknesses are net.

TURNED OAK DINING CHAIR

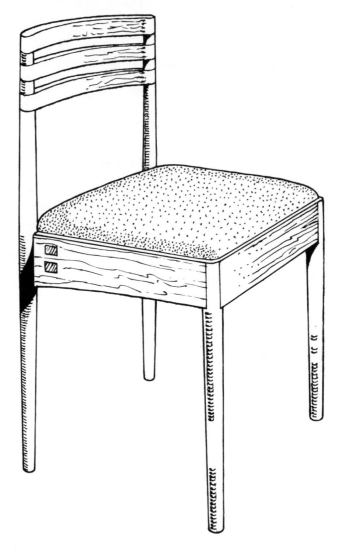

The essential features of this design are the turned legs which are all perfectly vertical. Slope on the back is achieved by having each back member of a different curvature, and the top rail is a smaller radius than the bottom one. Thus the back, while remaining vertical each side, slopes in the middle.

The degree of taper on the seat was arrived at by trial and error until it looked correct. You will notice that the seat is little lower than usual; its height is based on a British Standards recommendation of 17 inches. The 16½ inches from the floor to the top of the seat rail is based on the calculation that 1½ inches of latex foam will compress to ½ inch when sat upon, bringing the actual sitting height up to 17 inches. Anyway, it is comfortable!

Use oak if possible for this chair; it should be straightgrained, for the legs at least, as irregularly-grained wood does not turn well. Straightgrain is particularly necessary for the pins at the top of the legs which take the back members.

MARKING OUT
Finish the parts to the exact sizes given in the cutting list, making sure that all ends are square.

Cramp the backfeet side by side in the vice with their ends flush with each other, mark the mortise length and position, and square lines across both. Cramp and mark the front legs in the same way as the back, leaving a 'horn' (that is, some surplus) at the top of the leg. Square the mortise length on to both inside faces.

On the piece for the side seat rails, mark out the rails by means of a diagonal line as shown in Fig. 24.1, but don't saw out yet. Square a shoulder line all round at each end, and set a sliding bevel for the shoulder lines on the edges, and square across the faces of the front seat rail.

Now set the mortise gauge to the right setting for the front legs and gauge them, together with the front rail and the side seat rail piece. Reset the gauge fence so that the pins come centrally on the backfeet and gauge the mortise width on these.

CUTTING THE JOINTS
Chop the mortises in the legs. It's a good idea to plug the first mortises in the front legs with small pieces of wood planed to a hand-tight fit before chopping the second mortise, which meets the first in the leg.

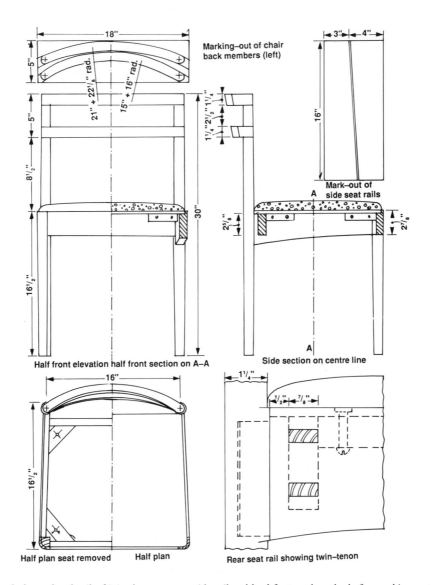

Marking-out of chair back members (left)

21" + 22⅛" rad.

15" + 16" rad.

18"

5"

5"

8½"

16½"

30"

1½" 2½" 1¼"

2⅝"

2⅝"

Half front elevation half front section on A–A

3" 4"

16"

A

Mark-out of side seat rails

A

Side section on centre line

16"

16½"

Half plan seat removed   Half plan

1¼"

½" ⅞"

Rear seat rail showing twin-tenon

Fig. 24.1. Elevations and plans; also detail of joint between seat side rail and backfoot, and methods for marking out.

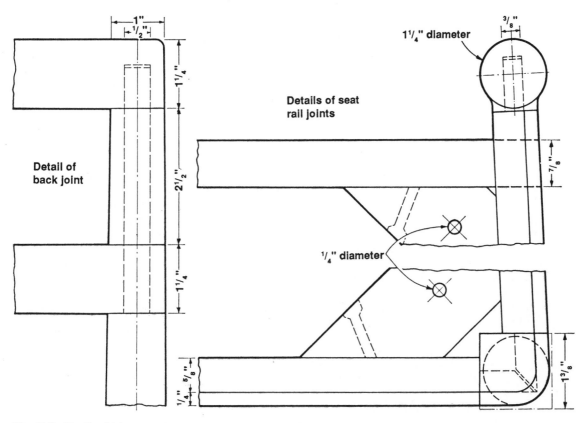

1"

½"

1¼"

2½"

1¼"

⅝"

¼"

Detail of back joint

Details of seat rail joints

1¼" diameter

3/8"

7/8"

¼" diameter

1⅜"

Fig. 24.2. Details of joints.

87

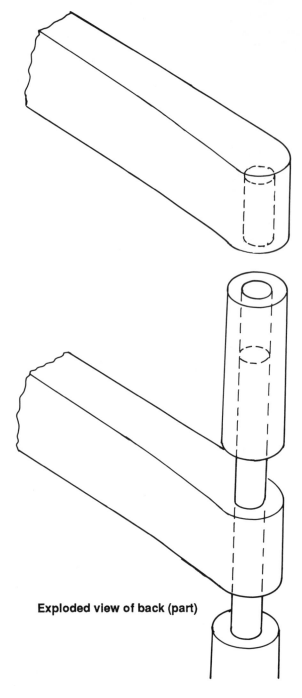

Exploded view of back (part)

Fig. 24.3. Exploded view of upper part of back.

This temporary plugging prevents the second mortise breaking out into the first.

The tenons on the wide piece from which the seat rails will be cut may best be worked with a rebate plane. Cramp a wide thin strip of wood, that has a straight edge, along the shoulder line; this is to guide the saw while sawing the shoulders. Then work down to the gauge line with your rebate plane.

You can now make the side seat rails by sawing to the diagonal line previously marked. Mark the tenon width to fit the mortises and cut them with a tenon saw. It may be better to saw out the tenons on the front seat rail in the conventional way, as the shoulders are not square. Tenoning is completed by cutting the twin tenons on the rear seat rail with corresponding mortises in the seat rail. Use the sliding bevel (as set for the front rail) to mark across the edges.

Finally, work the seat rebate on the top inside edges of the side rails and the front seat rail.

FIRST SUB-ASSEMBLY

Cramp up the side frames dry, without glue, and mark the rail widths on to the legs. Square lines right round the legs ⅛in above and below the rail positions; this marks the part which will be left square when turning. Then transfer the rebate position on to the front legs and turn them as in Fig. 24.4.

Next, saw across the inside corner of the front legs level with the rebate bottom and up to the rebate sides, as this makes working the rebate in the top of the leg easier after assembly.

Continue by polishing the inside faces of the side seat rails, masking out the rail position over the twin mortises. Then glue up and cramp the side seat frames and, when the adhesive has set, remove them from the cramps.

Fairing the side seat rails into the backfeet is a difficult operation to do well, so start by using a shoulder plane to produce a flat between the rail and the leg. Finish with a moulding plane or use a wide chisel, bevel side down, and work from the face of the rail towards the leg with a scooping action. You will need to remove the outside corners to continue the line of the leg, and a smoothing plane will do this easily.

Holding both side frames together in the vice, work the gentle curves in the under edge of the seat rails – a spokeshave is an ideal tool to fashion these very slight curves.

SECOND SUB-ASSEMBLY

At this stage, add the front and rear seat rails to the assembly. Cramp the parts together dry first, to check that all joints fit well. While the assembly is held tightly together, plane off any surplus from the ends of the through twin tenons.

Before finally gluing up, check that the outer face and under edge of the back seat rail, and the under edge of the front rail are all polished. Follow on by removing the cramps and finally gluing and cramping up. If possible, use softwood cramping blocks as any slight projection of the through tenons will bed into them and full pressure is thus ensured where it is needed.

THE BACK

While the first and second sub-assemblies are in the cramps, continue with preparing the back members and spacers.

Before cutting the sweeps, plot the hole centres so that they coincide exactly with the pin centres taken from the second sub-assembly. Bore these holes with great care as they must be exactly vertical. Next, cut out the back members, leaving about 1in extra on the ends. Turn both of the back spacers as a 'string', that

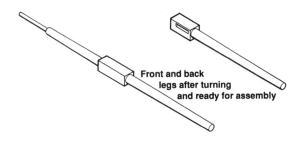

Front and back legs after turning

Fig. 24.4. Front and back legs after turning.

is, in one length. Part off to leave a ⅝in diameter in the middle. Rotating the work on the prong centre, feed in a ½in bit held in the tailstock. Saw the spacers to length, keeping the saw as close as possible to the spacer. Then polish them in the lathe before parting and drilling.

FINAL ASSEMBLY

Thread the back members and the spacers on to the turned pins at the top of the legs. Check that all is well, and glue and cramp up, with one cramp on each backfoot. When the adhesive has set, trim off the surplus from the back rails. Using saw and plane, finish off flush to continue the line of the leg. Spokeshave both faces of the back rails to give a slope in the middle of the back, using a round-faced spokeshave for the inside curve and a flat-faced one for the outside.

The heading illustration shows a chair with three back rails, but as an option you could make it with only two; for the three-rail version, make the spacers ⅝in long in order to retain the overall depth of the back. The radius of a centre back rail will, of course, be halfway between the radii of the top and bottom rails.

Continue the line of the turned front legs by planing off the outside corner of the square which was left on. To work the run-in of the rails into the legs, simply lay a chisel flat on the edge of the rail and push it towards the leg. In the same way, work into this initial cut by laying the chisel flat against the leg. Remove the 'horn' by sawing, allowing the top edges of the seat rails to guide the saw.

Working the rebate over each leg top presents a slight problem. Again, rest the back of the chisel flat on the rebate, and push towards the leg from both directions. Using a scribing gouge held vertically, work back to a carefully-drawn line and the rebate should be completed satisfactorily.

Saw the corner blocks from the length of wood given in the cutting list if they are marked out, so that every alternate block is the same way up. They should be drilled for screwing at the angle shown, and glued and screwed into position, with the top faces of the blocks lined up with the bottom of the seat rebate.

FINISH

Glasspaper the chair frame thoroughly, using a normal glasspaper block for the flat areas and outside curves, and a suitably-shaped block for the inside curves. The sculptured joint at the junction of the back leg and the side seat rail can be glasspapered to a good finish by wrapping the glasspaper around a piece of dowel rod.

The finish chosen was white French polish – this preserves the natural colour of the wood, and a pleasant satin sheen results if you use sufficient elbow grease! After the first coat is dry, which will take an hour or two, glasspaper it back thoroughly. Brush on a second coat and leave it overnight to harden completely; then rub it down well with the finest grade (flour) glasspaper, followed by fine (grade 00) wire wool to remove any surplus polish from the surface. Finish off by polishing with a soft white wax.

THE SEAT

Cramp the plywood seat base into the rebate. You have to be sure that the holes in the base are in alignment, so bore through the holes in the corner blocks, and fit the bolts and screws on the nuts. Cut round the nuts with a sharp knife, remove the seat base and chop the nut recesses to a depth of ⅛in. Glue the nuts into the recesses, using an epoxy resin adhesive.

Choose a softwood plywood for the seat base, as you will find it will take tacks easier than hardwood. Cut the base so that it has about 1/16in clearance all round in the rebate and, if a PVC cover is being used, bore four ½in diameter holes, one near each corner; these are to allow the foam cushion to breathe in use. Use a dab of upholstery adhesive in each corner to hold the foam on to the ply base.

Tack down right along under the front edge, working from the centre outwards, and do the same under the back edge, working the cover right round with the other hand before hammering in each tack. This imparts even tension to the cover; for the same reason pull it tight at the centre of the opposite side to where you are tacking. Continue working outwards towards the corner and get a tack right in the corner with the cover pulled tight. Finally, cut the surplus cover from the corner and tack down.

You can give a professional finish to the underside of the seat by covering it with black canvas or a similar fabric; turn the edges under and tack down all round.

CUTTING LIST

	INCHES			MM		
	L	W	T	L	W	T
2 backfeet	30½	1⅝–1⅜ dia		775	42–35	
2 front legs	17½	1⅝–1⅜ dia		445	42–35	
2 back rail spacers	6	1⅝–1⅜ dia		153	42–35	
2 back rails from						
1 piece	18½	5¼	1¼	470	133	32
2 side seat rails	16½	7¼	⅞	419	185	22
1 front seat rail	18¼	3⅛	⅞	464	80	22
1 back seat rail	17½	2⅞	⅞	445	73	22
4 corner blocks from						
1 piece	18	2	⅞	457	51	22
1 seat base, ply	18¼	15¼	¼	464	387	6

Also required: 1 piece pincore latex or plastic foam 18in× 15in×1½in (458mm×381mm×38mm); cover fabric 24in× 21 in (610mm×533mm); four 1¼in×¼in (32mm×6mm) dia brass bolts with slotted heads and matching nuts.
Working allowances have been made to lengths and widths; thicknesses are net.

Dining Chair

The design of this chair is in the contemporary style, particularly the seat (which is slightly lower than normal) and the sloping back rest designed to support the small of the back and give maximum comfort. It would look well in any hardwood but particularly in mahogany finished natural colour with birch dowel pegs as a decorative feature. In its method of construction it is similar to chairs of the Regency period, having two identical side frames connected by two curved back rails, two seat rails, and two stretchers.

As in all chair making, you will find that a full-size drawing is essential as most of the joints are slightly off-square, and you can prepare it from Fig. 25.1; only the side elevation and plan need be included. As much of the character of an elegant chair derives

from the careful shaping of the various members, three sections of the uprights A–A, B–B, and C–C are shown in Fig. 25.1 to serve as a guide. Some of this shaping can be done before the side frames are glued up, but the flow of the rails of the back rest into the back uprights (see part sectional plan, Fig. 25.2) will have to be done after final assembly.

SIDE FRAMES
These can be made first. The front and back legs taper in front elevation from ⅞in at seat level to ½in at the bottom. The back upright also tapers slightly in front elevation at the top, on the outside only, between the lower and upper rails of the back and you should work these tapers before shaping. Also, it is advisable to work the shaping of the top side rail,

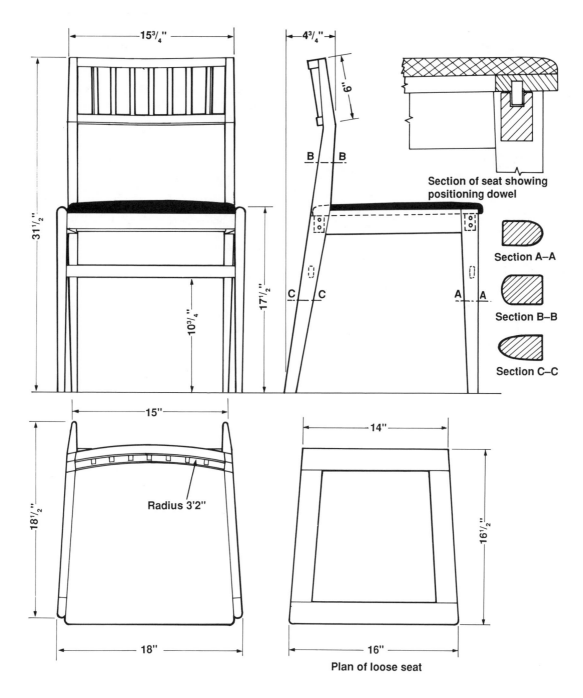

Fig. 25.1. Elevations, plans and sections.

see the front elevation, Fig. 25.1, before gluing up the side frames.

Use as large a tenon as possible between the side rail and legs when jointing up these side frames. The cross rails supporting the seat are through-jointed with ⅜in dia dowels so that the dowels peg the tenons and show as decorative details – you can wedge these dowels externally if you wish.

Next, tenon the two small 1in by ½in cross stretchers into the legs, taking care to scribe the shoulders of the tenons to the taper of the legs. Note that these stretchers have a flattened oval section.

BACK RAILS

The top rail of the back rest is curved to a radius of 38in, and the lower rail to a slightly smaller radius. Work the tenons of these rails square with the inside surface of the back uprights (see part sectional plan, Fig. 25.2) and shape the front and back surfaces of

the uprights to conform with the curve of the rails. Tenon the seven slats, each ¹¹⁄₁₆in by ⅜in in section, into the top and bottom rails so that their alignment coincides with the radii of the curved rails.

LOOSE SEAT

Make up the frame of the loose seat from 2in by ½in hardwood as shown in Fig. 25.1, using ¼in dia dowels for the joints. Remember when trimming this frame to allow enough room at the sides for the combined thicknesses of the webbing, covering fabric, etc. Webbing and rubberised hair will make an excellent seat, but you can, of course, use a plastic foam stuck to a ply base. The seat is held in position by a single ⅜ dia dowel let into the front of the frame and entering a hole in the front cross rail (see detail Fig. 25.1). Give extra strength and rigidity to the chair by gluing and screwing four corner braces to the side and cross rails as shown in Fig. 25.2.

91

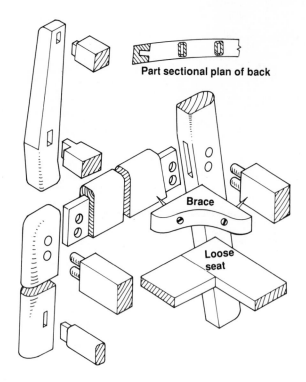

Part sectional plan of back

Brace

Loose seat

Fig. 25.2. Exploded view showing constructional details.

CUTTING LIST

	INCHES			MM		
	L	W	T	L	W	T
2 legs	20	2	⅞	508	51	22
2 backfeet	33	3	⅞	838	76	22
2 side seat rails	16	2¾	⅞	406	70	22
1 cross rail	16¾	2	1	425	51	25
1 cross rail	15	2	1	381	51	25
1 stretcher	18	1¼	½	458	32	12
1 stretcher	16	1¼	½	406	32	12
2 rails for back rest,						
each	16½	2½	¾	419	64	16
7 slats	6	¾	⅜	153	19	10
4 corner braces, each	3	3	¾	76	76	19
Loose seat frame						
1 front rail	17	2¼	½	432	58	12
1 back rail	15	2¼	½	381	58	12
2 side rails	13¼	2¼	½	337	58	12

Working allowances have been made to lengths and widths; thicknesses are net.

Chair with Hide Seat and Back

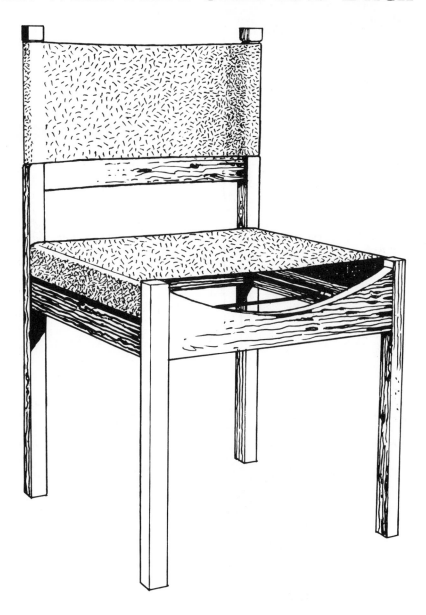

The essential feature of this design is that both the seat and the back are entirely separate units from the frame, and are not fixed to it permanently.

GENERAL REMARKS
The methods of tensioning the seat and the stool are identical; with the back, however, straining was considered unnecessary as it takes only 20% of the occupant's weight which is insufficient to cause any permanent stretching of the leather. Although the backfeet are straight and vertical (to maintain the rectangular appearance of the design), the back is surprisingly comfortable as the leather conforms to the sitter's back. What happens is that, when pressure is applied to the top edge, a see-saw action takes place and the lower edge comes forward to give support where needed.

LEATHERWORK: THE SEAT
We start with the leatherwork because the frame is conceived solely as a support for the hide, and not, as in other designs where the leather is added as an upholstered adjunct to an existing frame.

Choose leather of a good density, provided it is not stiff. It should be about 2mm to 3mm thick and cut so that its grain runs at right angles to the direction of pull; that is, from the front to the back.

Make paper or cardboard patterns of the seat and back from the plan in Fig. 26.2; these will enable you to mark out the pieces on the best part of the hide. Lay the pattern on the reverse side of the leather and mark round it with a ball-point pen. Cut out the shapes with a sharp craft knife, using a straightedge as a guide. Fold over the ends of the seat to a pre-marked line. Then mark a lap of about 1in and coat

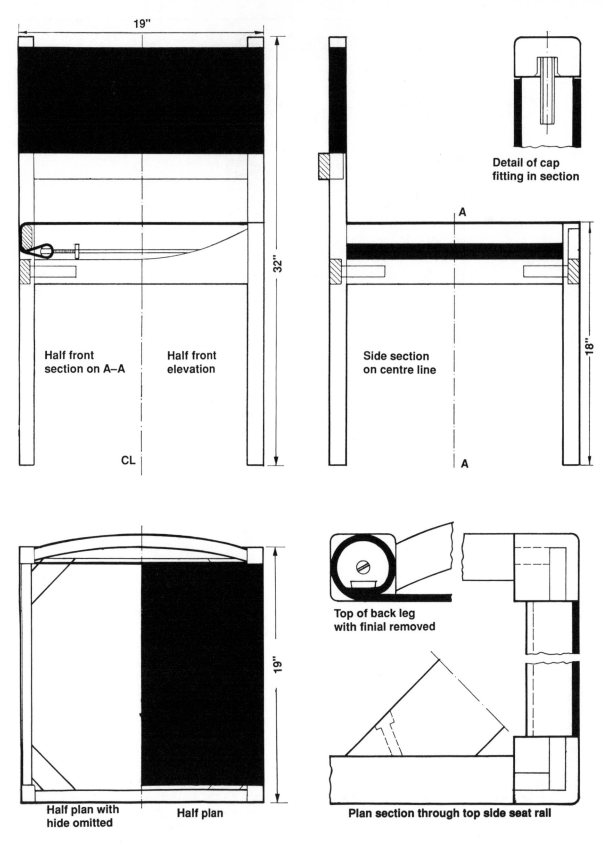

Fig. 26.1. Elevations and plans; also details of leg cap fitting, and section through top side seat rail.

it with a PVA adhesive of the type suitable for upholstery work. Cramp the work between two bearers until the adhesive has set.

This method on its own has proved to be satisfactory in the original but, if you are afraid that the seat might suddenly give way, a saddler will stitch the lap for a modest fee. Similarly, the dovetail-sectioned mild steel strips at each end of the back piece were fixed with an epoxy resin adhesive alone but, as an extra precaution, you can reinforce the glued joint with set screws or rivets.

Make the holes in the seat leather that allow the turnscrew to penetrate the straining bars by using a home-made device – this consists of a ½in dia mild steel tube ground on the inside to give a cutting edge. Use it in a bit brace, holding the leather in the vice with a thick piece of dowel in the loop (a broom handle will do).

94

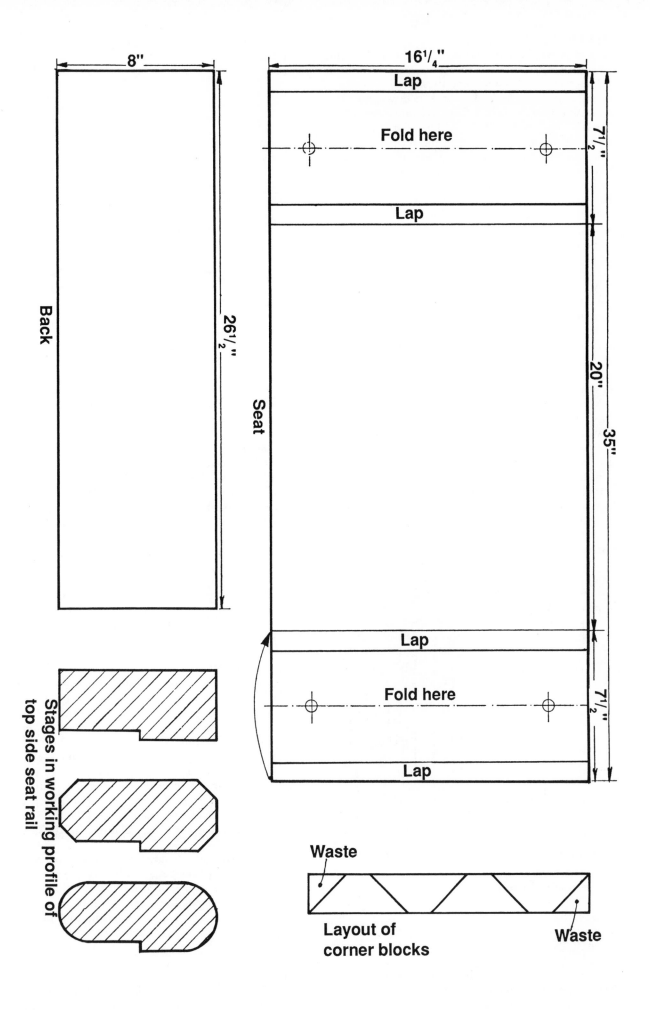

Fig. 26.2. Measurements of the hide seat and back; also sequence of working the profile of the seat side rails.

THE FRAME

Teak was used for the frame and makes a striking contrast if black hide is chosen.

The frame is designed specifically as a means of supporting the hide, and is broken down into two sub-assemblies, namely a front assembly and a back frame, Figs. 26.3 and 26.4. These are joined by means of the side rails to form the final assembly.

Cut mortises in the legs for the front and back rail tenons to a depth of ¾in only; this is to allow for mortising to a depth of 1in for each side rail tenon. This secures the greatest strength where it is most needed in a chair which has to resist a front-to-back strain. The detail drawings, Figs. 26.3 and 26.4, make the point clear. Similarly, mortise and tenon the top back rail 1in deep to achieve maximum strength.

An aid to marking the curved top back rail and the top edge of the front seat rail may be made from a thin lath, 1in wide by ¼in thick. Drill ¼in dia holes about 1in from each end of the lath, and pass a double thickness of string through one of the holes and knot the ends. Thread the loop through the hole at the other end of the lath and secure it by passing a short length of dowel through it.

You should now have something like an archer's bow. To produce the curve required, slip a piece of dowel or a pencil between the strands of the string and turn it like a tourniquet until the lath is bent to the required curvature. Primitive, but effective!

A further process which needs to be completed before assembly is working the top end of the back legs to take the leather. Cut the groove to house the metal strip first; you can best do this with an electric router. Alternatively, saw the sides by cramping on a strip which has been planed to the required angle to act as a guide, removing the centre waste by plough-planing. Chop a recess at the end of the proposed groove for the saw and the plough-plane to run into.

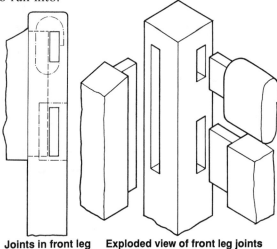

Joints in front leg   Exploded view of front leg joints

Fig. 26.3. Details of front legs and joints.

TURNING

This is the next operation and will increase the life of the hide back considerably as all sharp corners are completely removed. Using the impression caused by the plain centre as the hole centre, drill a ¼in dia hole to a depth of about 1in. This is best done on the lathe to ensure accuracy, but you can do it by hand if you are careful that the hole is drilled on the true axis of the leg. This hole is to take the ¼in dia

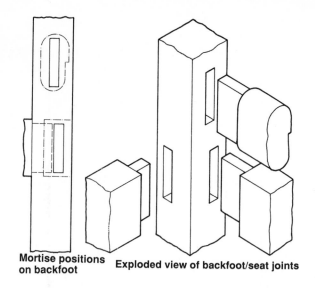

Mortise positions   Exploded view of backfoot/seat joints
on backfoot

Fig. 26.4. Details of backfoot and joints.

studding which is later screwed into place, Fig. 26.1. A slot sawn in the end of the studding will enable it to be turned with a screwdriver.

Assembly of the front and back frames may now proceed, after first ensuring that all inside faces are thoroughly glasspapered to a smooth finish.

SEAT RAILS

While the adhesive is setting, work the section of the top seat rails, and the best sequence of operations can be seen from Fig. 26.2. Use a rebate plane to produce the rebate for the hide, after which you can work the rounded edges. I marked each end of the rail by drawing round appropriately-sized coins. Then plane the corners off down to the line at an angle of 45 degrees; these and successive corners are removed until a true round is approximated. The final moulding is produced on the finished chair frame by wrapping a coarse garnet paper around the edge of the rail and pulling down on alternate ends in a to-and-fro action.

FINAL ASSEMBLY

This consists of gluing and cramping the front frame and the back frame together by means of the side seat rails. When the adhesive has set, remove the cramps and screw and glue the corner blocks into position.

The caps for the tops of the legs, Fig. 26.2, simply consist of a short length of teak of the same section as the leg. Fit a dowel nut into the underside of each cap, the nut having an internal thread which matches the studding in the top of the leg. You will need to bore holes to house the dowel nuts, and the diameter of each hole is equal to the core diameter of the nut's outer thread.

Now rub down all outside faces of the frame with garnet paper until you get a really smooth surface. Brush on a coat of boiled linseed oil, and follow with two or three coats of the same oil applied with a cloth. This should give all that is required of any finish, particularly if it is freshened up from time to time.

METALWORK

The straining bars are made from thin-walled ¾in o/dia steel tubing into which are welded tapped sockets to take the turnscrew, the bars being drilled with ⅜in holes at 2in from each end to take the sockets. Take great care to ensure that these holes are in alignment with each other.

The sockets are made from ⅜in dia mild steel rod. Drill along the axis with a tapping drill for a ¼in dia Whitworth thread; this is a coarse deep thread which is suitably strong for brasswork. Starting on the lathe, to ensure accuracy, tap these holes. Welding the sockets into the holes in the tube should present no difficulty as the thicknesses of both the socket and the tube wall are practically the same, and there should be equal and even distribution of heat and stress.

The brass turnscrew is threaded left-hand one end and right-hand the other. The adjusting wheel is turned on the lathe and is tapped with a right-hand tap; after screwing the wheel on to the bar as far as it will go, further movement is prevented by silver soldering.

For the metal securing strips on the ends of the leather chair back ½in by ⅛in mild steel was used, but doubtless almost any other metal would serve as well. The edges were filed to the same angle as the dovetail groove.

FITTING UP

When fitting the hide back to the frame, aim to enter the metal strips into the dovetail grooves almost simultaneously, and then be sure that the back is lowered into position at the same rate on each side.

Fit the seat by slipping the seat loops through the double side rail and inserting the straining tubes into the loops from the rear of the chair. Apply tension by means of the turnscrews which should be turned while each end is directed into its appropriately-threaded dowel nut in the straining tubes. The rate of turning for both turnscrews should then be equal and simultaneous.

CUTTING LIST

	INCHES			MM		
	L	W	T	L	W	T
2 back legs	32	1½	1¼	813	38	32
2 front legs	20	1½	1¼	508	38	32
1 front seat rail	18¼	4¼	⅞	464	108	22
1 back seat rail	18¼	2⅛	⅞	464	54	22
4 side seat rails	19	2⅛	⅞	483	54	22
1 top back rail	19	2⅛	1⅞	483	54	48
4 corner blocks from						
1 piece	15	2⅛	⅞	381	54	22
2 back leg cappings,						
each	1¼	1½	1¼	32	38	32

Also required: 1 piece of hide for seat 35in×16¼in×2 or 3mm (889mm×413mm×2 or 3mm); 1 piece of hide for back 26in×8in×2 or 3mm (660mm×203mm×2 or 3mm); these are exact sizes.

Metal fittings: 2 straining bars from thin-walled tubing, each 16in ¾in outside dia (406mm×19mm); 4 sockets from one rod 3½in×⅜in dia (89mm×10mm); 2 turnscrews, each 15in×¼in dia (381mm×6mm) brass rod; 2 turnscrew handles from one piece brass rod ¾in×1in to 1¼in dia (19mm×25 to 32mm); 2 back strips from two flat bars 8in×½in×⅛in (203mm×12mm×3mm) mild steel, brass, aluminium etc; 2 lengths of studding 1½in×¼ dia (38mm×6mm) for leg caps; 2 dowel nuts with internal dia ¼in (6mm) to match.

Working allowances have been made to lengths and widths; thicknesses are net.

Two Modern-Style Dining Chairs

The alternative designs show a chair with a show-wood back in the form of a figured splat, and one with an upholstered splat.

SETTING OUT

It is always advisable in chair construction to make a full-size setting-out drawing which includes a seat plan of the legs and framing, and on which you can superimpose the lines of the loose drop-in seat frame. In addition it's worth making a cardboard template of the backfoot so that you can mark out one inside the other to save timber. Notice, incidentally, that the backfeet are shown in the cutting list as 1in thick – the intention, in this one instance only, is that 1in stuff should be used to finish as full as possible, say 15/16in when cleaned up.

If you refer to the first illustration you will see that the grain of the seat frame runs right over to the extreme of the leg squares and at this point, you have to decide whether to introduce a fine knife-cut veneer to the front and end rails, or alternatively, glue and pin on solid facings (say 3/32in thick) mitred at the front corners.

Veneering is probably the better course, as the shoulder positions remain virtually unaffected. If you do use solid facings, you will need to make allowances for the thickness when setting out the seat plan so that the end rails, together with their facings, finish flush with the faces of the backfeet.

FRONT LEGS (A)

From the enlarged plan details given in Fig. 27.3, note that the turned shafts of the legs are set in 1/8in from the front and end faces of the leg squares, which means off-centering when turning the squares. The diameter of the shafts immediately below the squares should be 15/8in, tapering to 11/8in at the break of the toes, which are formed by recessing another 1/8in to the floor while maintaining the same line of taper. While each leg is in the lathe, give it a burnished finish with fine glasspaper to save work later.

From the setting-out drawing, gauge and work mortises in the leg squares for the tenons of the front seat rail, and follow on with those at an angle for the end seat rails. Alternatively, use dowelled joints if you wish, or tenon the side rails and dowel the front ones.

BACKFEET

In front elevation, these maintain a constant thickness which should finish 1in and certainly not less than 7/8in. When looked at from the end, aim for a width of 11/4in, and continue the line in a straight taper to 11/2in at seat frame level and thence to 11/4in at the base. The positioning and sizes of the mortises for the back end seat rails should be plotted with some care from the setting-out drawing so that you get maximum strength consistent with the amount of timber available. Certainly, the back rail will only need short tenons that butt against those of the end rails, which should be kept as near as is practicable to the outside faces.

SEAT FRAME RAILS (C), (D), and (E)

The front and end rails should be rebated to a width and depth of 5/8in to take the loose seat frame; the back rail has a rebate 5/8in deep and 3/8in wide. Note that the rebate edges finish flush with the faces of the backfeet as in Fig. 27.2, and then work tenons as necessary to enter the mortises in the legs.

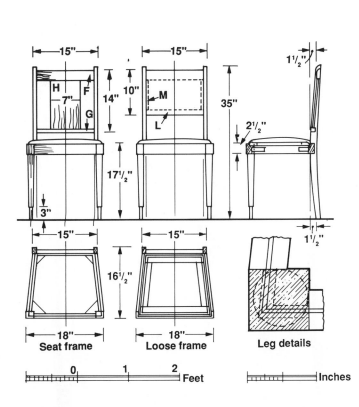

Fig. 27.1. Front and side elevations, with plan and enlarged section of leg.

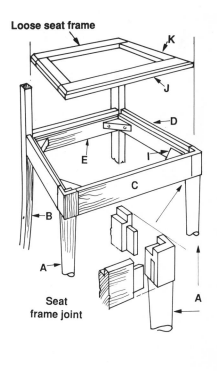

Fig. 27.2. How chair frame is made.

99

BACK FRAME RAILS AND SPLAT (F), (G), AND (H)

Fix the top and middle rails by means of stub tenons into the backfeet; you will also need to make grooves ¼in deep for the small tongues worked on the edges of the splat. The edges of the latter, being of veneered plywood, should be stained or veneered over wherever they show. Next, work the routed edge to the top rail and eventually shape the tops of the back legs to follow the same line.

The alternative upholstered back follows much the same construction. The top rail and the slightly wider middle rail should be tenoned into the backfeet. You will also need tacking fillets, which finish ⅛in below the faces of the backfeet and line up with the top and bottom rails. Screw the fillets to the inside of the backfeet to carry the braid or gimp which is tacked on later.

ASSEMBLY

Treat the back sub-assembly and the front sub-assembly as separate units before cramping them together to form the complete chair. That is to say, glue and cramp the three rails to each pair of backfeet and leave to set. Similarly, glue and cramp the front seat rail to the front legs. Continue by adding the side rails and testing for squareness and standing before the glue sets. Finally, glue and screw the seat braces I firmly in place, setting them down ¼in below the rebates into the angles of the frames.

LOOSE SEAT FRAME, (J) AND (K)

Make the completed frame to finish with a ⅛in gap all round inside the rebated frame rails – the gap is, of course, to accommodate the upholstery. Cut the end rails to the required length and dowel them between the front and back rails; then glue and cramp them together and, when set, plane a chamfered edge all round to gauge lines scribed ¼in down from the top faces and ½in across them. This ensures a soft edge to the upholstery.

CUTTING LIST

Part	INCHES L	W	T	MM L	W	T
A 2 front legs	19½	1¾	1¾	495	45	45
B 2 backfeet from 1 piece	37	4½	1	940	115	25
C 1 front seat rail	18	2¾	1⅛	457	70	29
D 2 end seat rails	16½	2¾	1⅛	419	70	29
E 1 back seat rail	15	2¾	1⅜	381	70	35
F 1 top back rail	15	2½	⅞	381	64	22
G 1 middle rail	15	1¼	⅞	381	32	22
H 1 splat	13	7½	⅜	330	191	10
I 4 braces from 1 piece	12	3½	⅞	305	89	22
J 2 loose seat rails	18	2¼	¹³⁄₁₆	457	58	21
K 2 loose seat rails	12	2¼	¹³⁄₁₆	305	58	21

For the chair with the upholstered back, omit (G) and (H) and substitute:

L 1 lower rail	15	1½	⅞	381	38	22
M 2 tacking fillets	9	1½	½	228	38	12

Working allowances have been made to lengths and widths; thicknesses are net.